Zen and the Cross Country Skier

Zen
and the
Cross
Country
Skier

by Dan Blackburn
and Maryann Jorgenson

Ward Ritchie Press
Pasadena, California

Library of Congress Catalog Card Number: 76-16266
ISBN: 0378-08952-8

The charts on pages 91 and 105 are courtesy
of Recreational Equipment, Inc.

The cover photograph is courtesy of Eliot Porter.
All the photographs in the book are by the authors.

PRINTED IN THE UNITED STATES OF AMERICA

To those who enjoy the outdoors in its many forms.

The Journey

Fundamentals of Cross-Country Skiing

"A ski trip is one of the most refreshing escapes from work one can imagine . . ."

The story of cross-country skiing is as big and beautiful as all outdoors. It abounds with excitement and beauty, and best of all, there is a tranquility that gives one a rare opportunity to think and listen to the voice from within. How does one condense all this into one small book?

As every aspect of life falls under the control of the computer tapes and punched cards, everybody and everything is forced into a niche. Books are not immune to this ultimate regimentation. Librarians explain that only by standardized categorization can they determine the proper shelf to which a new publication must be assigned. Thus, I am asked to describe what kind of book this is.

Is this a picture book with descriptions of an outdoor recreational activity? Yes, to be sure. But it is hoped that it will be even more.

Is this a "how-to-do-it" book for a sport rapidly increasing in popularity? While also true, this description relates to only one aspect of the text and photographs.

Then surely this must be one of those "self-improvement" guides aimed at helping the reader achieve greater understanding of the meaning of life through some philosophical concept. Yes, in part, it hopefully is this also.

When word gets out that you are writing a book, all of your friends (if only to make polite conversation) want to know the title and what it is about. Invariably my answer triggers another question: "What on earth does Zen have to do with the purely recreational activity of cross-country skiing?" As with most deceptively simple questions, this is a very difficult one to answer. Only by gliding swiftly on narrow skis across a frozen white wonderland twenty miles from civilization and feeling like the only human being on the face of the earth can one find the answer.

There, without the distracting background noises of civilization, your inner sensitivities and awareness have a chance to function. It is as close to a state of inner contemplation as modern man is likely to get. The old trees and timeless rocks seem to have a message if you only listen. The birds that fly overhead and the few animals still stirring in winter that scamper about the snow are as important as you are. Each is a link in a chain that makes up the universe. You feel suddenly spiritually enriched as though you have just discovered an eternal truth. For the first time you comprehend the true meaning of life. Such an inner awareness is an important precept of Zen philosophy.

If *Zen and the Cross-Country Skier* must be classified under a single category, then it should be thought of as a love story built around the developing relationship between two skiers and the winter world about them. It is the story of an ever-expanding awareness of the special magic that exists when Mother Nature casts her snowy blanket over the land.

Like many love stories, this one is formed by a triangle. The two people whose skiing adventures provide the thread that ties it all together make up two sides of that triangle while the natural splendors and sense of community with the surroundings combine to make up the third side. I believe we are well qualified to tell such a story—I with my typewriter and Maryann with her camera. We have backpacked in the summer and fall and skied in winter and spring. We have never ceased to feel a sense of awe at the serene peace and beauty. To truly commune with nature is to expand one's horizons beyond the scan of eyesight alone. There is a certain sense not unlike the feeling you can get in those magnificent old cathedrals of Europe. In the wilderness, splendid peaks rise like mighty spires while buttes and plateaus stand as proud altars.

It has been said that every book should have a purpose. This one is no exception. We come as disciples seeking converts. We hope to lure other city dwellers out of their snug caves of urban hibernation during the winter months and into the great outdoors. There, where the silence is so intense that you can hear a pine needle fall onto the snow, awaits an experience whose impact may last a lifetime. In such a place, under such conditions, and given pause for introspection, you may gain fresh insight into the mysteries and ever absurdities of life. A Zen teacher once said that the search for universal truth is expressed in such terms as:

> If you look for it, you cannot see it
> If you listen for it, you cannot hear it
> If you believe and embrace it, it is inexhaustible.

And that, in essence, is what this book is all about.

The
Journey

"It was January before snow conditions enabled us to keep our first date with our new love . . ."

Whenever people become interested in a sport, they always seem to find and keep returning to a favorite sports shop. With salespeople usually highly experienced and knowledgeable about the sport as well as the gear, such stores serve not only as sources of equipment, supplies, and information, but they become meccas for people who share the same interests.

It was during a season-end sale at one such shop five years ago that we were first introduced to cross-country skis. Initially Maryann and I had started hiking and backpacking in order to remove ourselves from the routines of daily life. As time went on, the challenge of the wilderness and the desire to experience its beauty became stronger and stronger, and we needed proper equipment. Thus, for the need of a particular strap, we arrived at Kelty Mountaineering at the end of the summer.

They were setting up the displays of the winter sports equipment in the store, and I think it was Maryann who first spotted the long, narrow strips that looked like skis. We wondered why they were so different from downhill (or Alpine) skis. Our curiosity attracted the salesclerk, who presented us with a detailed description of the art of cross-country (or Nordic) skiing. While he continued his monologue, I examined the binding that held the boot to the ski. It was beautifully designed and attached so that it held only the toe of the boot, allowing the heel to rise and the foot to perform a walking or shuffling motion.

Driving home that evening, we discussed the skis and what they could mean to us. Every time we had been to the mountains in winter, we had watched the skiers, who seemed to spend more time lining up and waiting for the lift than they did sliding down the crowded slopes. It all seemed too urban and mechanized for our taste.

I guess that was the real key to our enjoyment of backpacking—the desire to be removed from other people. We realized that the narrow Nordic skis could be used for such cross-country trips in winter. Once we learned to maintain our balance, we could gradually acquire the ability to manipulate them successfully with a pack on our backs. When we mastered the ability to ski with a full load, just as in hiking, we could go on backpacking trips twelve months of the year. This was something we simply had to learn more about.

During the nights that followed, we read all the pamphlets that we had collected at the sports shop. Within a week we had committed a great deal of the information to memory. Only one thing kept us from dashing out the very next weekend and trying our hand at cross-country skiing—there was no snow. In spite of our eagerness to get into cross-country skiing, that little four-letter word (snow) loomed large on our horizon as an inescapable prerequisite.

During the seemingly endless weeks that we waited for the first snow to cap the upper elevations of the nearby mountains, we read everything we could find on cross-country skiing. The pickings were slim. Even the main branch of the public library offered only two meaningful books on the subject. Written many years ago, both books were hopelessly outdated, and they either dealt with

16

advanced techniques or were aimed at the highly experienced Alpine skier who wanted to try Nordic skiing. They didn't even mention the modern fiberglass skis. In spite of these obvious drawbacks, we did glean some information from the books and learned the fundamentals of the basic stride and the mechanics of getting safely up and down a hill, slowing down, and stopping. Armed now with at least preliminary information, we were more anxious than ever to put it to use.

Perhaps the most encouraging thing we learned from our research was that cross-country skiing is much less dangerous than downhill skiing, even for the amateur. We had seen many weekend skiers hobbling around the office on crutches, and we were cautious, but such serious accidents are almost unheard of among cross-country skiers. Under most conditions you will never approach the speed of a downhill skier, and about the worst thing that could happen is that you will lose your balance and fall down a couple of times until you get the hang of it. A fall in a level field covered with soft snow may bruise the ego, but the body will remain intact.

It was mid January before the snow conditions enabled us to keep our first date with what was to become a new love. Our destination in the San Bernardino Mountains required a two-hour drive. Earlier in the week, we had gone to Kelty's and reserved a complete package of rental equipment consisting of skis, boots, poles, bindings, and selected waxes. A friend who was experienced in both downhill and cross-country skiing had agreed to join us and provide some basic instructions to get us started. After a quick stop to pick up the equipment and lock the skis and poles into the ski rack on top of our friend's car, we were off to the snow.

While our reading and conversations had given us a basic sense of what we were supposed to do on cross-

There was a touch of irony to the situation in which we found ourselves. The arrival of snow had always meant the end of the backpacking trips we so enjoyed. Winter seemed to be the most desolate time of year, when nothing grew. Life seemed to be suspended, trees became skeletons, animals disappeared, and the snow made walking almost impossible. Now, with our new-found interest, we began to pray for the white stuff.

I pride myself on my nonconformity and my ability to be a detached observer. Each year when others around me would bemoan the fact that the snows were late and had ruined their plans, I remained aloof. The only real enjoyment for me was the opportunity to escape from the crowds through backpacking. But now my nonconformity was shattered; I had joined the crowd anticipating the first snow

country skis, it seemed as though some personal instruction would be a good idea. It is true that the basic elements of cross-country skiing can be learned from a book and we have put many book-learned techniques into practice. But some personal coaching is very helpful and seems to add an extra amount of confidence that books seldom produce. Many places offer group lessons and we were fortunate in having a friend who was willing to take time out for some individual instruction.

In any event, we had been looking forward to this weekend introduction to cross-country skiing with growing enthusiasm. Weekends have become an important institution in today's world. We seem to be structured to fill the time between Friday and Monday with activity totally different from that which keeps us occupied the rest of the week. The weekend was originally designed as a period of rest and rejuvenation to prepare for the forthcoming days of work. Now, many people seem to use the weekend for a furious outburst of activity that leaves them more exhausted — at least on a physical level — than the regular work week. Perhaps we are becoming a change-of-pace culture in which escape from everyday activity is the weekend goal.

It was possible to almost feel the questioning glances from the people in the other cars who clearly were wondering what kind of skiing we planned to do. We weren't too sure ourselves, but we were about to find out.

Certainly, the patches of snow that began to dot the sides of the road as we wound our way into the nearby mountains provided a change of pace from the puddles of oil and patches of broken glass that lie along the shoulders of the freeways. Most of the people in the cars both ahead of and behind us were headed for the downhill resorts and our car with the skinny cross-country skis on the roof seemed almost out of place.

We pulled up to a small parking area that obviously saw more use in summer than in winter. The snow-covered meadow where we would begin our acquaintance with cross-country skiing lay about fifty yards away. We slipped out of our shoes and pulled on the light-weight touring boots, tugged the skis and poles from the ski rack, scooped up the package of waxes and trudged to our starting point.

The bright sunlight literally danced off the snow on the meadow and once we were away from the road the silence became a tangible thing. There was no conversation. We inhaled the fresh, cold mountain air in deep gulps as though trying to purge our lungs of the Los Angeles smog. The far side of the meadow sloped upward into a series of hills, and beyond them the ridge of the San Bernardinos could be seen. But, most of all, it was the quiet, a warm, welcoming quiet, that gave the meadow its character.

Even before the first step could be taken on the skis, wax had to be applied to the bottoms. The wax permits the skis to slide forward smoothly while gripping the snow to prevent sliding backward. At least, that's the theory. In practice, it is really a combination of wax and skiing technique that does the trick. Different waxes are designed for different ski conditions. Some waxes can be sprayed on but most of them require rubbing in with a cork or, in the case of the very sticky klister waxes, spreading on with a piece of plastic that comes with the wax. When you are ready to put away the skis, the wax is removed with a special scraper or through the use of other special sprays that dissolve the wax. Many people also use Coleman fuel as a convenient wax remover. They simply pour a film of it over the bottom of the ski and rub the wax off with a rag.

On this first time out, we quickly discovered that rubbing in the wax takes some patience and a lot of elbow grease. Our friend explained that we did not have to get the wax perfectly smooth but that we should try for a fairly thin, even cover. It sounded easier than it turned out to be and we were later to learn about skis that require no waxing at all. But, by then, waxing seemed a natural thing to do.

Finally, we laid out the skis on the snow, pushed the toes of our boots into the bindings, locked them in place and were ready to begin. Our friend began with a sort of shuffling step and I stepped out in his track. Two shuffles later I hit the deck. I had leaned too far forward and the skis had simply shot out from under me. A few minutes later, Maryann managed to perform the same inelegant maneuver. It was the sort of shared experience we would rather have done without. But every journey must begin with a first step no matter how shaky or uncertain.

We continued with a slow and easy approach, taking shuffling strides that were as short and cautious as an infant's first attempt at walking. Our friend had carved a circle in the meadow and our task was to follow in his tracks. The circle looked awfully big as we made the first circuit but it shrank in size as our confidence grew.

We had had enough experience at other sports to realize that bad habits are easy to make but extremely difficult to break and so we cheerfully accepted the suggestion that we start out the hard way by learning to keep our balance on the narrow skis without the use of poles. Had we used them at the outset, we might have been tempted to rely on them as crutches to maintain our balance. The poles have a very definite role to play in cross-country skiing on both flat terrain and on hilly climbs where they provide extra leverage—but all that comes later and not at the very beginning.

The first taste of what lay ahead with the long, narrow skis was enchanting. This was to be a new and invigorating experience in a world already filled with excitement. There was no question but that we would eventually embark on a long cross-country trip. But first we had to learn to ski with a backpack loaded with all the items necessary for such a trip into the winter wilderness.

This initial exposure to cross-country skiing was focused on the basics—developing a proper stride, getting familiar with the skis, attempting some simple hill climbing as well as skiing back down and generally getting a feel for the mechanics of the sport. And it was mixed with moments of simply pausing and enjoying the surroundings, basking in the pleasure of just being there on that snowy meadow.

Subsequent weekends were spent returning to the meadow and eventually venturing on to other spots recommended by friends and by members of the Far West Ski Association. We also solicited advice on where to go from members of the U.S. Forest Service on the theory that they should be familiar with the national forest areas. For the most part, that theory proved out pretty well.

Of course, much of the success of any long, or even relatively short trip, into the wilderness in either summer or winter depends on the preparation for it. Perhaps I am a bit of a stickler for preparation. Obviously, the preparation of news reports, which I do on a daily basis, involves factors of time, delivery, clarity, and presentation as well as some forethought. To a degree, it is a work syndrome that carries over into all phases of my life. We all have such traits that provide the guidance that we feel is necessary to sustain us.

Whatever the forces at work, it was evident that not only would simple skiing proficiency be required for any long outing into the winter-wrapped back country, but some experience with winter camping and snow survival would also be essential. This meant preparation, attention to detail, and some short trips on our own—trips that would serve to further deepen our enthusiasm for this Nordic gift to winter activity.

A scientist would probably relate these traits to the genes from which one is created. There is a frightening concept offered by some scientific prophets who claim that they are on the verge of controlling the mix of human genes in such a way as to be able to create a person with a prearranged personality. Would that creation really be a person? Science fiction writers have long predicted a society that would include genetically programmed people who would be assigned certain tasks related to their levels of efficiency. There are already hints of that forecast in our current society although they have occurred through social conditioning rather than a genetic plan.

21

"A halo rimmed the moon, which glowed dimly through the clouds like a spotlight on a frosted window . . ."

Our first overnight excursion on cross-country skis was off to spectacular start. At this rate, by morning the snow clouds would deposit several inches of dry powder on the slightly crusted base that had slowed us down. Tomorrow's ski conditions promised to be ideal, and we would be able to travel fully twice the distance we had covered on this day.

Shortly after our evening meal, we had taken time to enjoy the sheer delight of skiing by moonlight. A cloud had obscured the moon, and the blue-white snow glowed under the light of the galaxies spread above us. It had been a memorable experience.

This was the final phase of our self-instruction course to prepare us for the great adventure we were planning. By working overtime two nights last week, we had wangled Friday afternoon off. Our gear was already packed, and by 1:30 P.M. we had arrived at the lodge that was to be the starting and finishing point for the triangular course of our first trial run, many more were to come.

Now, the tiny snowflakes reflected the light of the moon as they wafted slowly down to earth. The only sound to break the silence was the snapping of dry twigs in the smoldering campfire. At such times it is easy to

In the soft moonlight the broad meadow and the hillside beyond emerged as a two-color mural of green and white. The whole world seemed to have become a living Christmas card. At such moments, alone in this majestic setting, Maryann and I might be the only people on earth.

Last night had been totally different. The sky had been crystal clear with thousands of stars twinkling down from the heavens. It was as though we could see to the very ends of the universe. In the city one tends to forget how many stars there really are. To the average urban dweller, such a panorama is limited to a planetarium, where tiny rays of light are projected onto the darkened dome of the ceiling by complex optical systems, while a prerecorded soundtrack describes the spectacle. Only in the wilderness, staring up into the heavens, can man truly contemplate the universe and realize the infinitesimal role he plays.

The vista before us was one of unspoiled splendor. The freshly carpeted white fields were bordered by the rich tapestry of evergreens against the rugged green and brown background of the towering pines and cedars. The virgin snow was marred only by the tracks of a few scattered rabbits and field mice. It was one of those days that is the answer to a skier's prayers.

A sense of self-satisfaction, tinged with a touch of smugness, permeated my consciousness and touched my ego as I lay quietly, waiting to be overtaken by sleep. I though of those who limit their skiing to the crowded downhill slopes and spend their nights huddled around roaring fires in steam-heated ski lodges with their people-packed bars and restaurants, the din of conversation, and the blare of a raucous juke box. Such an atmosphere may be fine for those who feel secure only in a

drift into self-reflection. Maryann must have felt the same, because she also was immersed in inner thoughts.

Inside the snow cave that we had constructed around the trunk of a fallen pine, we sat in snug comfort as the outside temperature edged its way down into the teens. A cup of hot tea warmed us inside while the parkas we wore staved off the chill outside. Zipped snugly into our sleeping bags we would sleep soundly and comfortably in temperatures that the uninitiated would be certain would freeze us to death before dawn.

In the morning we were awakened by the soft glow of sunlight filtering through the transluscent roof and walls of our snow cave. We swept away the fresh layer of snow that had partially blocked the entrance to our shelter. It had taken more than two hours to build our snow cave, so we decided to leave it intact. Perhaps other cross-country skiers would find and use it.

After depositing a three-inch layer of dry powder on top of the crusty base during the night, the snow had stopped. The sky was clear and blue, and the sun shone brightly. Before it rose much higher, we would need sunglasses to cut its glare on the bright new snow. The temperature had risen to the upper twenties. It would be necessary to guard against sunburn as carefully as on a July afternoon at the beach.

On the small backpacking stove that I always carry with the rest of our camping gear, we heated water for hot chocolate from foil-wrapped packets. After breakfast we took turns trudging off behind a clump of nearby bushes with the roll of toilet paper that is a vital part of the Nordic skier's pack. Baring the buttocks in the icy weather is not the frighteningly uncomfortable experience one might imagine it to be. The fatty tissue of that part of the anatomy is well designed as insulation against the cold.

24

We stuffed our sleeping bags tightly and stowed the rest of our gear into backpacks and then helped each other strap them on. We mounted our skis, grabbed our poles, and were off for our first full day of winter backpacking on cross-country skis. In order to beat the Sunday traffic, we planned to get back to our base by 2:00 tomorrow afternoon. Today, Saturday, was the only full day of skiing we would have.

There is a thrill in making the first trails in fresh snow that only an ardent skier can fully appreciate, and with two quick strides we glided out onto the meadow, cutting tracks into the snow. We charted our course by means of my ever-present compass and topographical maps, which directed us toward the nearby woods and beyond into open country.

I felt a twinge of embarrassment at this momentary display of sentimentality, which is generally regarded as a sign of emotional weakness in a man. Then I remembered the words of my jiu-jitsu instructor: "The greatest strength lies in an open display of weakness." During those lessons in the martial arts, he had planted the seeds of the philosophy of Zen in my mind. Now, after years of lying dormant, those seeds were coming to fruition.

The weather and skiing conditions were so ideal that we reached the checkpoint that marked the end of the second leg of our triangular course a little after 2:00 P.M. Yesterday, it had taken us nearly two hours to construct our snow cave. Another approach to shelter in winter is to build an igloo. We had read about it and were anxious to give it a try, but not today. It was too perfect a day for skiing. I had brought along our backpacking tent, with its collapsible fiberglass poles and windproof, waterproof fabric. It could be set up on a prepared site in a matter of minutes. Because our main objective for this stage of field training was to get in all the practice we could on cross-

mob scene but, like us, a rapidly growing number of people are discovering the joys of quiet forests and snow-covered meadows that can be reached only atop narrow cross-country skis.

Overhead, a pair of sparrows darted back and forth just above us. There seemed to be something friendly in their antics, as if they were providing us with aerial cover and reconnaissance, lest these newcomers become lost. Birds are among campers' best friends in the outdoors, providing weather forecasts, music, and playful fun. Suddenly, out here in the frozen wilderness, I saw them in a new light. As far as my eyes could see, to the horizon all around, they and we were the only living creatures in sight. Why, of all places, had they elected to flit about just above us? Were they perhaps playfully planning to use us as moving targets for their droppings? My mind rejected the brief thought, and I suddenly felt ashamed for having had it. After all, they were nature's creatures, the same as we are. Who was to say which of these two pairs of living things was more important? Because the path ahead was clear for several hundred yards, I found myself staring up at them as if seeking a sign, an answer.

Some inner awareness, shaken from a long-imposed lethargy, seemed to sense the answer. It was as if they were saying, "See, we fly across the sky on wings while you fly across the snow on skis. We're not really so different from one another, are we?"

country skis, we decided to use the tent. During the remaining hours of sunlight, we back-tracked and practiced on a few of the steeper inclines we had passed.

We were back at our second checkpoint an hour before dark. Our previous camping and skiing experience had put us in good stead for our first experience at tenting down in the open snow. We had selected the location because it seemed like an ideal campsite. There was a stream of fresh water nearby that would save the time and fuel required to melt snow for water. The spot was reasonably level, and it was shielded on two sides by dense growths of tall trees that would serve as a windbreak. We were careful not to erect the tent under or too close to the trees. Falling snow and limbs could easily collapse the fragile structure.

We tamped the snow down with our skis over an area slightly larger than the floor of the tent. Then we removed our skis and stomped the entire area with our boots into an even more tightly compacted base. We had had lots of practice at setting up the tent, so it went up quickly and smoothly. We arranged it so that the entrance faced the windbreak provided by the trees to keep out chill winds.

The day had been beautiful, even balmy at times, but at this time of year the temperature could drop sharply after sundown. Instead of building a campfire outdoors and allowing the cooking heat to escape, we decided to cook inside the tent on the backpacking stove. Our tent had a cooking hole, with a zipper flap near the main entrance. This would allow the smoke to escape but later could be closed to trap some of the heat and raise the inside temperature. Just before sundown I took a light-weight collapsible plastic bucket (a handy item in any backpack) and went down to the stream and filled it with fresh clear water.

It had been a long day and we were exhausted, not from strenuous activity, but rather from the sheer exuberance of the experience. We sat quietly, each of us reliving in his own mind the experience of spending two days and nights in the frozen wilderness. Modern civilization, with its problems and frustrations, seemed a million miles away. I felt physically and emotionally cleansed and revitalized. The cobwebs were all swept away from my mind, and I could face the week ahead. I contemplated my feelings when the sparrows had "escorted" us. Perhaps it was an example of what some people call cosmic consciousness.

Maryann and I spread out our sleeping bags, making sure neither of them touched the side walls of the tent. If they did, the warmth of our body heat against the cold surface of the tent could cause condensation, which could freeze.

Sunday dawned as bright and clear as the day before. With any luck it would turn into an instant replay of that perfect Saturday. With the exception of our skis and poles, we had dragged all our gear inside the tent to keep it as dry and warm as possible. After a quick breakfast we broke camp, loaded the gear into the backpacks, and were off on the final leg of our last basic training mission.

By now we by no means knew all of the answers, but this self-instructed training had at least given us a base from which to learn the finer points. The final part of our triangular route took us over some steeper and more rugged terrain than we had yet encountered. We took it slowly and calmly, but the going was tougher by far than the day before, and we would overshoot the original arrival time by at least an hour.

During the last hour of our approach to the lodge, we were on reasonably level ground. Here and there we passed other Sunday afternoon Nordic skiers who pre-

That night as I rested, comfortable and well fed, I thought about people who were lost in the snow and eventually, when hunger become an overwhelming passion, were confronted with the possibility of having to eat another human being in order to survive. I don't think any person could rationally comment about what he or she would do under those circumstances, but I wonder about myself. My values make this act unthinkable. But which one of the forces in my body—the hunger or social values—is the strongest? We learn more and more about ourselves every day; yet in the long run we know very little. When we are confronted with a question of this magnitude, we have no answer, only speculation.

ferred the open fields to the crowded slopes. A family of four waved a friendly greeting as we passed about ten yards apart. The youngsters were way out ahead of their parents, handling their skinny skis as if they had learned to walk on them. Closer to the lodge we encountered a group of young people. The boys wore only the briefest of shorts and the girls as little more as the law allowed. Their bodies were richly tanned, giving them the healthy glow usually associated with surfers on the beach rather than skiers in the snow.

We were tired but happy as we loaded our gear back into the car. We were also ravenously hungry. Driving home after a good meal, the glow of excitement from the two days of cross-country skiing made me think of ways we could turn around and stay in the mountains. There are some people who have the opportunity to structure their lives so that they are able to do the things they really want to do and live in the places they like best. Most of us, however, are committed to a society that demands regular appearances and scheduled productivity from its members. Maryann and I fall into the latter group. We both work in the same business but for different companies and never take any of our business world with us to the mountains. I guess that is the real purpose for taking these trips: a complete separation in mind and body from daily routine. In the projected futuristic society with genetically programmed people, I imagine that the need for this separation could be removed from the body. If that were the case, however, I'm sure these new people would develop other problems and would need attention in much the same way we seem to need these trips.

We had come a long way in the four years since we had first heard of skinny skis and learned about wintertime backpacking and camping trips on these narrow cross-country boards. In the beginning we fell down a lot but kept up our spirits by laughing at each other's clumsy antics and trying to learn from constant mistakes. There were times when it was all pretty frustrating. But the goal we had in mind made us grit our teeth, set our chins, and keep trying.

The first time or two we stuck pretty much to level ground and concentrated on trying to remain upright, rather than flat on our butts. And it wasn't long before we were able to remain upright for at least the major portion of the time and to maneuver from a preselected Point A to Point B.

During the second winter we gained a little more self-confidence and began to climb up and slide down some of the steeper slopes. Our progress was slow because of the limited time we could devote to this new-found recreation. We had a four-hour round-trip drive between home and the snow. Often other demands on our time made it possible to only devote one day of an ideal weekend to our self-instruction program.

Fortunately, we were able to enhance our own efforts under the coaching of instructors at one of California's smaller but better cross-country ski schools. Former Olympic skier Gunnar Vatvedt's highly regarded Viggo Nordic Ski School in Hope Valley, California, put a lot of extra polish on our abilities and broadened our skills in winter camping and survival. A true son of Norway, Gunnar's English may have its rough spots but his skiing speaks eloquently on his behalf.

One weekend we spent Saturday night at one of the ski lodges. It proved to be, for us, a disastrous experience. We had come up to the snow to get away from the crowds, noise, and smog of the city. At the crowded lodge it was as though the city had come with us.

Midway into the second winter season we began to learn to adjust our balance on skis to carrying packs on our backs. If we were ever to take the long trip we had in mind, we would have to learn to ski with a 40-pound backpack strapped to our shoulders. We started off with small daypacks containing just an extra sweater and the camera equipment. It was like having to learn to balance ourselves on the narrow skis all over again. Gradually we began to increase the load. By the middle of the season, we could ski carrying a full backpack.

We had heard about Joe Leonard, a well-known Idaho mountain man and director of the recently formed Leonard Expeditions. He had established a chain of ski huts in the lofty Sawtooth Mountains, north of Sun Valley. Here, he took small groups of experienced skiers on snow safaris in some of the most magnificent mountain terrain in all of North America. We had worked hard to attain the required proficiency. Our weekend outings had satisfied us that we were at last ready to embark upon the great adventure and had given us a sample of what it would be like. But they couldn't approach the pleasure of the longer expedition, as we were soon to learn when the long-anticipated adventure became a reality.

"Nothing would prevent us from embarking upon the backpacking expedition that filled our dreams . . ."

The skiing season was rapidly drawing to a close. Bright spring sunshine and early rains had caused the snow to thaw and turn mushy. Only the highest elevations now offered satisfactory ski conditions. Most of these required too much travel time for our limited days off. The daily announcements of ever-rising temperatures assailed our ears like the death rattle of winter, of which we had grown so fond. It was time to pack away the skis and plan for next year — the year we would try for a really long trip, an expedition.

As the gray skies of the California mountaintops gave way to clear blue, storm clouds gathered far to the east over the nation's capital. One of the greatest political scandals in American history was slowly being dragged from under an oval rug and subjected to the full light of public scrutiny. These were dark and dreary days that added disclosure upon disclosure until the total effect was one of physical and mental numbing for those who reported each development and those who watched and listened in shock and dismay.

As a sound engineer for CBS, Maryann's work schedule increased proportionately to my own. Weary as we were from the long hours and constant tensions, however, we managed to get in regular periods of exercise to keep in

31

The tree line falls behind as a skier pushes upward along a slope that sweeps toward a mountain peak.

shape for the dream experience which, although relegated now to the back of our minds, was never quite extinguished. On a few blessed occasions we were even able to take a day off. Tired as we were, we would be up at dawn, load our backpacking gear into the car, and be off for the high country. It was a cathartic experience that did us more good than sleeping around the clock. Here, we were able to cleanse our minds with the crisp clean air and refresh our spirits with the beauty and balance of nature. It was a great consolation to observe that in this unspoiled wilderness the inflexible laws of nature were strictly and sincerely observed. Even in a world distorted by false standards and values, there was still something in which man could put his faith and trust.

The months passed with dizzying speed as we were caught up in events that did not seem real. The world we had known seemed to be breaking into a series of shattered illusions, as though we were viewing the whole scene through a kaleidoscope. The Fourth of July and Labor Day approached and passed as though in mockery. I could scarcely believe that fall was upon us. Winter and snow would follow just as rapidly.

A friend working on a political campaign finally handed us the key to our desires. I had been chatting casually with Senator Paul Laxalt of Nevada about the upcoming presidential campaigns and our conversation had turned to other subjects. We began to talk about skiing and I argued the case for cross-country skiing and suggested that someone who represented the state of

Proving that cross-country skiing is not reserved for the young, a senior skier and his dog cut a trail in San Bernardinos.

The well-known Mammouth Mountain of California—long a favorite of downhill skiers — is seen through the trees as a cross-country skier approaches from the back side of the peak.

Nevada should be more familiar with the sport. The next day my friend telephoned and asked if I were familiar with the Sawtooth Mountains of Idaho. "Only by reputation," I responded.

Then, she told me about Joe Leonard. In Idaho, Joe Leonard is a celebrity. He is the reincarnation of the legendary mountain man. Somewhere, in another life, he must have been a travelling companion of Jim Bridger. What my friend had to say was that Joe Leonard had formed Leonard Expeditions. In the summer, he would take people kayaking on the wild rivers. In the winter, he would take them into the Sawtooths on skis.

The key to Joe's idea is a special "hut" system. Before the first snows fall, he sets up a series of canvas tents large enough to accommodate eight people at one time. Then,

34

with the assistance of licensed guides, he takes skiers into the Sawtooths using the tents as base camps. This was the first season for Leonard Expeditions and it was still in the shakedown phase with many bugs yet to be worked out. But the idea seemed like one whose time had come.

The hut system for cross-country skiers is an old one in Europe but has never really been put into practice in the United States. An attempt was made at it not long ago in Colorado using abandoned miners' cabins, but it was never really formalized. The idea makes a lot of sense. By utilizing the huts (or tents) as base camps, it is possible to lighten the load carried by skiers because the packing of tents for individuals or couples becomes unnecessary. In addition, it makes it possible to cache food more easily. Camping conditions remain fairly rugged. The tempera-

A solitary ski trail cuts its way through the forest in a typical southern Sierra setting in the Rock Creek area not far from Bishop, California.

35

The forest of Sequoia National provides winter solitude for the cross-country skier.

ture still plummets at night and the wind still howls around the corners. It is hardly civilization but it does permit greater flexibility.

Maryann and I kicked the idea around for a while and agreed that it sounded like just what we were looking for. With that, I picked up the telephone and called Joe Leonard at his home in Stanley, Idaho. He answered more questions about his expeditions, and I answered his questions about our experience and skiing ability. What we finally agreed upon was to organize the longest trip to date into the Sawtooths utilizing Joe's system of tents. There were a series of telephone calls back and forth as we ironed out the details and agreed on what we would bring as compared to what Joe would provide. Because we were carrying heavy camera equipment, it was decided that Joe would add an extra guide to pack food supplies that would otherwise have been divided between Maryann's and my packs.

The hardest part was to match up available dates and Joe, with his unfailing courtesy, finally maneuvered his schedule around so that it could meet the less flexible schedule imposed upon Maryann and myself by the nature of our jobs. After that, everything else was easy. Plane reservations were made and the important checking out of all our equipment got underway. It was a step-by-step process that was designed to insure a safe and successful as well as memorable trip. We also spent a fair amount of time studying maps of the area.

The Sawtooth Mountains lie due north of the famous downhill ski resort area of Sun Valley, which is renowned for its exceptional powder. As one drives north from Sun Valley, the Sawtooths rise impressively above the Stanley Basin, which serves as the jumping off place for summer backpacking trips into the surrounding wilderness. These days the Stanley area is fast becoming a ski touring and

Cross-country ski expedition leader Joe Leonard pauses along a wilderness trail.

snowmobiling area as well, with the accompanying antagonisms between those who seek the solitude of the winter wilderness under their own power and those who seek to overpower the wilderness with engine noise and gasoline fumes.

Environmentalists from throughout the United States have joined in a long, hard-fought battle to preserve the rugged wilderness of the Sawtooths from the encroachment of the everpresent land developers. While the fight to save the natural integrity of this primeval land has left its political scars, it has left the mountain range unspoiled. The effort was crowned with success when the Sawtooth Recreational Area was established — a development that brought the mountains under federal protection. Many of the permanent residents of the Stanley Basin approve of the result and, while none of them will grow wealthy off the land, many people will be able to join them in admiring and enjoying the area in its natural state. The environmentalists who seek to preserve this remote area are not satisfied with the current status and want to move one step further by having the Sawtooths declared a national park. At this point, the outlook is promising.

We also learned from that that another giant step had been made for ski touring. Ever since the advent of the sport, the U.S. Forest Service had looked upon cross-country skiers as a potential source of trouble and worries. Many enthusiastic but ill-advised skiers would take off on a cross-country trek alone, it was feared, and when they failed to arrive at their predetermined destintion on schedule, the Forest Service would be called upon to undertake extensive, and expensive, search operations. A lone skier suffering from exposure twenty miles from the nearest source of aid can be a hopeless case. Teams of two skiers are not much safer. If one is critically hurt in the wilderness, the other is physically unable to carry him out. All he can hope to do is to make his companion comfortable and warm while he skis back for help. More often than not, he becomes disoriented and is unable to guide the rescue party back to his injured companion. Small wonder that members of the Forest Service viewed such winter sportsmen with a jaundiced eye.

Organized ski tours, like those directed by Joe Leonard, do much to change all this. No fewer than three skiers ever made a cross-country trek, so if one was hurt, the other two can bring him out. In larger groups the chances for fatal accidents are reduced even more. As a result the Forest Service realized that the winter sportsmen need not

A mid-day camp in the snow at 8000 feet on the approach to Quadrant Mountain.

be a source of worry and it now condones and helps in the planning of carefully supervised activities in the areas for which they are responsible.

The attitude of the Forest Service people was not difficult to understand. The sad job of bringing out the "big losers" fell to them, and it was far from an enviable position. In addition to the danger of skiers getting lost or seriously injured far from civilization, there was the totally unpredictable weather to contend with. Sudden blizzard conditions, sleets, hails, or freezing rains could come on without warning. Often these would bring with them sudden darkness, even at midday. This would make it impossible for the skiers or search teams to erect the time-consuming igloos or snow caves as shelter, and the high winds near hurricane level that often accompanied these sudden high-altitude storms would make it virtually impossible to erect a tent. The only protection from the elements would be to burrow into the snow like a group of sled dogs.

Thus, it was clear that Joe Leonard's hut system met a very real need from the standpoint of both the skier and the Forest Service ranger alike. In many ways, it looked like a cross-country skier's dream of heaven and, now, we were about to share in it.

"As our trip grew closer, the days seemed to grow longer . . ."

We had packed and repacked our gear until we had almost worn it out from sheer handling. There was no detail, however slight, that we hadn't checked and double-checked.

The trip upon which we were embarking would last six days and five nights—the longest winter cross-country ski trip into the Sawtooths thus far. Having the licensed Idaho guides take the responsibility for transporting the food supply would make a tremendous difference. The hut system made it unnecessary to carry along our own tent, and this too would be a saving grace.

For the cross-country skier, the backpack checklist is as vitally important as the pretakoff checklist is to an astronaut. Once in the frozen back country, you can't just pop into a corner drug store and pick up something you may have forgotten. In the wilderness little things can often assume major proportions. A forgotten pair of sunglasses, bottle of suntan lotion or aspirin tablets can easily ruin an otherwise awe-inspiring experience. Neglecting to bring along some sort of insect repellent on a summer backpacking trip, for example, can prove disastrous.

The night before we departed we ran down our checklist for the umpteenth time. If there were anything we had forgotten, it simply wasn't on the list. We locked our backpacks and boots in the trunk of the car. The skis and

41

poles were standing just inside the front door. We were as ready as we would ever be. The only thing we needed now was a good night's sleep.

We were in high spirits as we battled the freeway traffic to the airport. Even the lane-switchers and the last-moment mind-changers did not annoy me this morning. We purposely arrived an hour before flight time. This, too, was totally out of character for me. I usually have to run to make the plane. The porter unloaded our gear, and Maryann went to the check-in counter while I parked and locked the car and walked back to the terminal. We stepped on the moving ramp through the tiled tunnel that led to the loading area. At the top of the escalator, we checked the location of our boarding gate and went into the restaurant overlooking the airfield for a hearty breakfast — another rarity in my day-to-day routine.

Our eagerness to renew our minds and spirit in the great sanctuary of the Sawtooths made the smooth flight from the commercialized "City of Angels" to this lofty Valhalla seem fully twice as long as it actually was.

At last the "Fasten Seat Belts — No Smoking" signs flashed on, and we began the sweeping descent to a smooth landing on the runway of the Twin Falls, Idaho, airport. I remember thinking at the time that it was like a long downhill ski run onto level meadows at the base of a mountain.

As we stepped from the plane, the crisp, clean air was like a window suddenly opened in a smoke-filled room. The total absence of smog and poisonous industrial gases was immediately apparent. The thin, icy air had an invigorating bite and a slightly intoxicating effect on us, as we were accustomed to the thicker atmosphere at sea level. In the Twin Falls terminal, an effervescent young woman approached us and introduced herself as Sheila Leonard, Joe's wife.

42

Once our luggage and gear was loaded into the Jeep, we piled aboard as Sheila took the controls for the three-hour drive to the Stanley Basin, the headquarters and jumping-off point of Leonard Expeditions. The long, winding drive to Stanley took us through some of the most rugged terrain in North America. We passed within miles of the Craters of the Moon National Monument. Here, it would not take an overactive imagination to believe that one had been magically deposited on the moon.

In spite of its rustic simplicity, the home base of Leonard Expeditions was the most thrilling vacation spot we had ever been. Just forty miles due west of Borah Peak, the highest point in Idaho, it was banked in deep snow. We would spend today and tonight here, gradually becoming acclimated to the higher altitude—always a good idea in the high country. Tomorrow morning, with the other members of the expedition, we would be off on the grand tour of the Sawtooth huts.

That night Sheila and Joe prepared a festive dinner party that not only served as a get-acquainted session, but provided the last full meal for the five people who would embark together on the great adventure early tomorrow morning.

The first day dawned on a bleak note. A grey sky wrapped itself around the mountaintops amid clear indications that bad weather might be in the offing. Nonetheless, hopes were high as we strapped on our backpacks and tightened down our skis. One after another, we climbed a small embankment near the road about a mile from Stanley and struck out on the trail that would take us to the first of the huts, where we would spend the night.

The trail to the Sawtooth Lake hut winds along Iron Creek and rises about 500 feet in the last mile, with the hut itself at the elevation of about 7000 feet. Within an

I suppose one might say that we were hardly taking on a raw expedition, as we were bringing along many of the comforts of home. That may be partly true, but our society has schooled us to accept such arrangements. White hunters in Africa engaged troops of natives to care for them on their safaris so they could concentrate on the pleasurable parts of the trip only. Although I would have liked to go into some uncharted area —someplace that had never been traversed by man—I know that such a thing would have been impossible and unsafe. The sense of accomplishment I require can be satisfied under safe and controlled arrangements made ahead of time.

hour of starting, a light snow had begun to fall, and there was little doubt that those early clouds would deliver their unwelcome promise. By the time we had put a couple of miles behind us, it became necessary to stop and rewax, as the wet snow was making conditions much too slippery for the hard wax on the bottom of our skis.

The first leg of the trip was designed to give the guides a sense of the abilities of the different skiers in the party so that the group did not wind up in terrain too difficult for some of those taking part. In the case of our group, that posed little problem, as we were all experienced cross-country skiers. For us the first six miles offered an opportunity to limber up muscles and readjust to skiing with an unwieldy pack on our backs. We skied at a casual pace and arrived at the hut within three hours, just in time for lunch.

The huts are really canvas tents that can be torn down easily in the spring and removed so that summer hikers find the area in its natural state. Each hut has eight rope-and-canvas bunks tied to wooden frames that serve as part of the skeleton for the tents. There is also a wood-burning stove, which provides both warmth and heat for cooking, although the cooking is more often done on a Coleman stove set up in each hut. Sometimes a bottle of brandy is found tucked away. Uncorked, of course, it seldom lasts long.

Once we had dumped our packs and consumed a lunch of fresh fruit, cheese, and salami, we stepped onto our skis for a short trip to nearby Alpine Lake. The afternoon outing had a twofold purpose: first, it would provide everyone with an opportunity to become familiar with the avalanche equipment and, second, we would all have a chance to practice some downhill skiing.

The Sawtooths are very much avalanche country. The steep mountain slopes and heavy snow pose a real threat

44

Use of Nordic skiing's Telemark turn helps a skier cut through the trees on a downhill mountain slope—skiing down.

to the unwary or inexperienced skier. In fact, the avalanche threat is a major reason to have any tour accompanied by experienced guides who know the most hazardous avalanche areas and how to avoid them. But even with guides, some areas can't be avoided completely, and caution is essential. In our case, the arrival of fresh snow added to the danger.

The traditional piece of avalanche equipment has long been the avalanche cord, which trails out behind a skier crossing a dangerous slope. But Joe Leonard offered something more sophisticated. He equipped every mem-

Cross-country skiers check a topographical map as they chart their trail in the winter wilderness.

ber of the party with Austrian-made Pieps Motronic transceivers instead. The electronic beeps that the transceivers emit can be heard over a 60-foot radius, providing a quick and effective guide to any buried skier. Before we left the hut area, we spent a half hour practicing with the Pieps equipment. Joe would hide one under the snow and then we would all search for it by turning our transceivers to "receive" and homing in on the sound of the beeps. Maryann quickly proved to be the most adept, and we decided to keep her near the front at all times so that she could help find anyone behind her who might get buried. Fortunately, we never had to put her skill to the test.

The climb toward Alpine Lake involved a 600-foot elevation gain and the crossing of two large avalanche areas. At each, the five of us spread out sixty feet apart and crossed one at a time. We could hear the snow groan and shift, but no slides occurred. Before long, we had reached the lake area and were ready to practice downhill turns on the route back — a route that wove its way among the trees and made sharp turns almost mandatory. As is usually the case, the return trip took far less time than the climb up to Alpine Lake, and it wasn't long before we were all assembled back at the hut. There, hot lemonade was enhanced with a splash of whiskey as we relaxed and swapped stories.

One unique item in the first hut deserves special mention. Unlike the other huts, where the stoves provided the heat, the Sawtooth Lake hut was equipped with a cast

At day's end, wilderness skiers gather around a hot, tin stove in a mountain's hut.

A trio of cross-country skiers forges its way through a winter storm.

iron stove. It weighed at least ninety pounds, and Joe Leonard had carried it in on his back. He says it took him nearly two days before he could straighten up after that effort, and he vowed not to repeat the experience. It was the kind of thing we had learned to expect from Joe — something beyond what anyone else would do.

Within hours, it was clear that one debate was likely to be unresolved on this trip and would indeed be the sole bone of contention among us for the entire six-day period. The Californians and the Idahoans split irrevocably over the question of klister waxes. The Californians — including Maryann and myself — held firmly to the view that klister is a last resort that adapts poorly to changing conditions. We argued vehemently in favor of

Swix yellow—the wax that works so well in the variable conditions of a California spring that it has been dubbed the "California crud" wax. But the Idaho contingent held out for the klisters, and we were to yield reluctantly to their arguments on several less than memorable occasions.

The next morning brought the first real challenge of the journey—getting out of bed. The temperature had dropped to zero, and crawling out of a warm sleeping bag was not easy. Almost as an afterthought, we had stuffed down socks into the foot of the sleeping bags, and they helped ease the chilly transition from sleeping bag to tent floor.

The first priority was to get a fire going in the stove. Have you ever tried to light a match at 6:30 in the morning when your hands are shaking from the cold? The first couple of tries were unsuccessful, but soon small flames began snapping their way among the twigs that served as tinder. Once the stove became hot enough, a skillet crammed with bacon was placed on top, and it wasn't long before the mouth-watering aroma of bacon and eggs permeated the hut. It may not have been *haute cuisine*, but it was hot and tasty, and it hit the spot.

The day's agenda had only one item on it—a rugged climb to Sawtooth Lake. A hearty breakfast was part of the preparation because we were going to need all the energy we could get. In terms of distance, Sawtooth Lake wasn't far—only about four or five miles from the camp—but there was an 1800-foot elevation gain, including a ridge at the 8600-foot mark that had to be scaled on foot, not skis.

The early stages of the tour were not difficult. We had covered part of the route the day before during the journey to Alpine Lake. The climbing was fairly steady but involved crossing one major avalanche area. We

I recall these encounters with a mixture of distaste and irony. I cannot, for example, quite settle the matter in my own mind— how it could have been that we five, all mature and sensible, could have permitted such an argument to jar against the setting in which it occurred. In a manner of speaking, I suppose one could say that using the proper ski wax might mean the difference between life and death under certain exacting conditions, but that would be stretching matters completely out of proportion. The truth lay in another direction. Here we were, as close to nature and self as we were ever likely to get, and yet we had been contentious, arguing over what amounted to very little. It was as if we had been clustered around a desk in an office, heatedly debating next year's budget, wrapped up in commercial concerns.

checked our electronic avalanche equipment carefully and spread apart more than fifty feet as we made individual crossings. At one point, a threatening crack from a nearby slope sharply raised the level of tension, but fortunately the snow stayed in place.

The trees began to thin out, and the twists in the trail became increasingly abrupt as we wound our way higher toward the ridge that we would have to scale on foot. Finally it became evident that the time had come to remove our skis and hike the remaining fifty yards to the top of the ridge. The terrain had become too rocky and steep to permit the use of skis. The skis and poles became climbing tools that helped us maintain our balance as they gave extra leverage to our straining arms, which pulled us upward.

At last, we reached the top of the ridge. It had been a very long fifty yards, but once we caught our breath, we realized the view was worth the climb. The Stanley Basin lay spread before us. To the east the snow-capped White Cloud Mountains rose in rugged splendor while the Sawtooths wrapped themselves around us. The minutes floated by as we took in the panorama that nature had provided. From our vantage point it seemed as though we were looking down on a sea of snow that drifted through the green forest below and emptied onto an open beach that was the Stanley Basin. Reluctantly we broke the spell and pointed our skis toward Sawtooth Lake, which lay an easy half mile or so away.

A bright blue sky had added to the beauty of the trip thus far, but a rising wind brought the first wisps of clouds that hinted at a grey afternoon. The lake itself was frozen over and would remain so for many weeks. We found a rocky outcrop jutting above the lake and settled down for a leisurely lunch. The cheese and salami washed down with fresh mountain water tasted very good, and we luxuriated in the warmth of the sun while gazing down at the frozen lake. Peace settled over us, and it yielded only slowly to the knowledge that we would have to start back to camp.

More clouds were blowing in, and the temperature had begun to fall as we stepped into our skis and strode out toward the ridge that we had climbed earlier. Once again it was necessary to remove our skis in order to scramble down the rocky slope, but climing down was much easier than climbing up. Although we soon left the rugged ridge behind us, the return trail remained steep and treacherous as it wound its way among the trees. The snowfall had been scanty in recent days, and the famous Idaho powder was missing. As a result, the snow was firmly packed, and we tended to gain speed much too quickly. For the most part, we opted for long traverses that lengthened the distance traveled but reduced the hazard of a serious spill among the trees. We ended with a final sprint across a meadow on the edge of camp.

It was a tired crew that settled in for dinner next to the cast iron stove. The warmth of hot tea spread throughout our tired bodies, and there was no doubt that we would sleep well that night. Before we rolled into our sleeping bags, Joe Leonard talked optimistically about the hut system. At 37, Joe already has a substantial reputation both as a summer kayaker and a winter mountaineer. He is committed to making his hut system a success. As he explained, "This is the thing I enjoy doing. I've worked at many other things, but I decided this was what I wanted to do. I really love it. I never get tired of going into these mountains." We nodded sympathetically.

A chilly grey overcast greeted us the next morning as we shook ourselves from our sleeping bags and prepared for the next leg of the trip—a six-mile jaunt to Goat Creek camp. The journey included a 900-foot elevation

And therein lay the other half of my reaction —the distaste. Now that I think about it, it seems that the chief aim of man is to assert himself, with or without reason. The greatest of wars have been fought over trifles, even over such misunderstood things as honor. But all of these things clear out in nature. No one can ignore the message of nature, if he permits himself to hear and see it.

I remember looking carefully at Joe at this point. I suppose I envied him, at least in the way we envy those who represent something we know we can never become and whose lives are of a completely different cut from our own. Joe, above all, was living his life assertively. He was asserting that he was an individual, that he renounced the urban jungles, that he disputed mankind's rape of the earth, that he was one with nature. Utterly unpretentious, totally practical, completely absorbed in what he does and who he is, Joe has gone beyond competing with other humans. He gives them the space to do what they do and be what they are, those very tenets of his own life, but beyond that, he has come to a finely tuned appreciation of what matters and what doesn't. This is best characterized, I believe, by a story he told me about himself. Some years ago he had occasion to come to Los Angeles on business. He made it as far as the San Fernando Valley, took a good look around, decided his business wasn't that important, and made a U-turn. He never got to Los Angeles; his business, whatever it was, it still waiting.

In a way, Joe typifies the person one might meet in the mountains. It isn't fair to believe that he is out of touch with things, because he isn't. But he is the sort of person who discriminates between different orders of the same simple thing. He sees a mountain adventure as being exactly what it is; he doesn't elevate the experience to a

gain and normally would not have posed many problems. But these were not normal conditions. As we shouldered our packs, the snow lay wet and heavy beneath our skis, and the temperature was erratic. After some debate, we decided to try purple klister as the running wax for the day. It was a disaster. In fact, nothing worked well. Under these conditions, the merits of waxless skis could be seen.

We slogged along under conditions that quickly produced exhaustion. Ordinarily, cross-country skiing is not terribly difficult, but when snow conditions are really adverse, just sliding the skis forward can become a chore. It took us three and a half hours to reach Goat Meadow, where we paused for lunch. It was obvious that stormy weather was on its way. The wind was blowing, and there was a muggy hint of rain in the air. We hoped it would become snow. Damp and disgruntled, we finally arrived at the hut, where we shed our wet parkas and donned wool sweaters. The weather was depressing.

Nonetheless, we decided to attempt a trip to Goat Falls. The view is said to be beautiful, but the snow conditions ranged from bad to terrible. No wax seemed to work well, and we finally fell back on the California standby—Swix yellow. It may have been just our imagination, but it seemed to work a little bit better. Unfortunately, the weather deteriorated even further, and more travel became impractical. We finally abandoned the trip to the falls. At the rate we had been traveling, it would have taken much too long.

Back at the camp, we broke out the new Mountain Safety Research stove. The stove generates a high degree of concentrated heat from almost any liquid fuel, regardless of the outside temperature. It boils water rapidly and meets all cooking needs. It can also serve as a torch for stripping wax from skis. By the time we had put it

life-and-death struggle against hostile elements (even when it is), nor does he downgrade it to a nuisance better accomplished by helicopter. Walking or skiing across mountains is not so much a "trip" as it is a pilgrimage, even though a pilgrimage is supposed to lead somewhere. Joe's pilgrimages, for him, lead to a heightened spirit, an intangible perception of self that is neither egocentric nor analytical. It is always a spiritual adventure for Joe, although I think he might argue the point. Even though he doesn't compete with other humans, he does compete with himself, and that is altogether different. He tries steep slopes, seeks extreme altitudes, forever testing how fast he can go. In a way he looks the part: eyes steely blue, hair prematurely grey, a long moustache, medium build—on the wiry side— and a deliberateness of action that makes for few false moves. He conjures up a vision of Hollywood's strong, silent types. But he has a sense of humor and can be drawn out.

A giant fallen tree offers a place to rest and improve the wax job on the skis in Sequoia National Park.

53

Three skiers take on the challenge of Lassen as Eagle Peak looms ahead of them.

through its paces, there was general agreement that it is an exceptional outdoor stove. (It is also expensive.)

St. Patrick's Day dawned with some blue sky in sight but with many clouds floating around the edges of the horizon. It was clear that we were going to have to abandon one of our goals — photographing cougar. Any tracks that might have been useful had been thoroughly obscured. Furthermore, we were facing the toughest part of the tour with the prospect of poor weather conditions to add to the difficulty.

The six miles to be covered that day included a 1000-foot elevation gain and the prospect of more avalanche hazards on top of bad snow conditions. Under the circumstances, a debate over which wax to use was inevitable. With many reservations, it was decided to give purple klister another chance. If nothing else, the decision highlighted the problems that can confront the back-country skier. These problems do not detract from the special joy of skiing wilderness areas. Rather, they demand a willingness to recognize that the meadows, mountains, and forests have their own rules and do not adapt to the whims of temporary visitors. The goal becomes finding what works best with nature rather than struggling against the surroundings of the moment.

On this day we started out in wet snow on which the purple klister worked quite well. But it wasn't long before we were winding our way among the trees where the snow lay deeper, colder, and drier. The result was that the snow quickly clumped on the bottom of the skies, making them heavy and awkward. Then, almost as an after-

An old wooden bridge provides passage toward the mountains at the south end of Jenny Lake.

thought, it started to rain. Fortunately, we were climbing more or less steadily. At the 8500-foot level, the rain changed to wet, heavy snow, and the going really got tough.

What it all added up to was the clear fact that no single wax was going to see us through this part of the journey. The purple klister had failed and even old, reliable Swix yellow was having its problems. In all, we made a total of four stops for rewaxing. The best combination turned out to be a mixture of blue and purple klister and Swix yellow. It may not have been the ideal technique, but it worked, and when skiing the back country, what works is what counts.

Finally, we crossed a ridge at 8600 feet and traversed a heavily wooded 100-foot slope to the Marshall Lake hut. It had taken a party of experienced skiers five hours to cover six miserable miles. No one would boast of that record, but by general agreement, it had included some of the worst conditions any of us had ever experienced.

As we relaxed in the hut, a loud rumble was heard from the nearby slopes. The storm had eased, and we decided to abandon the shelter of the hut in favor of a trip up a steep ridge to see whether an avalanche had come down. The question was never answered because a combination of fog and low-hanging clouds moved in from the west and hampered visibility. The effort offered other rewards, however. We discovered a series of small bowls nearby and put in a couple of hours practicing downhill runs and polishing turning techniques before returning to camp.

By nightfall, a high wind had whipped the sky clear of clouds, and a bright moon bathed the landscape in a soft, clear light. It was obvious that this would be an extraordinary opportunity for a moonlight tour. We waited until the moon was up fully and then stepped out on our skis to enter a vastly different world. The sky overhead became a private observatory filled with millions of lights. The constellations stretched across the sky with a clarity never seen from city streets.

The shadows of the trees reached like giant fingers across the trail and often plunged the forest into darkness that prevented any rapid skiing. No one wanted to ski into that darkness without knowing what might be buried there. But no one was in a hurry. The winter woods at night offer a special sense of solitude that is too pleasant to let any thought of hurrying on to another destination interfere. Robert Frost's words — "The woods are lovely, dark and deep" — sprang easily to mind.

Almost without thinking, I drifted off from the others as they stood wrapped in their own thoughts. A low ridge about thirty yards away offered a solitary vantage point from which to take in the snowy evening. It drew me slowly to it with an irresistible pull that seemed to move my skis without any physical effort from me. It was as though the forest and the mountains had taken control.

As I reached the ridge toward which my skis had carried me, the wind rose slightly and began tossing small snowpuffs into the moonlight. I could hear it sighing over the snow and murmuring around the swaying branches of the trees. At first it seemed as if a dozen tiny voices were whispering in the mountain air. Then, they seemed to speak as one.

I paused and shook my head. This was no time for silly fantasies. The moonlight made it clear that I stood alone. Still, I felt as though I was being addressed. I recalled Schopenhauer's reality ("anything we perceive to be real") and Russell's ("substance is no test") and the answer came to me as clearly as if it had been spoken. Reality *is* experience. If I were experiencing a voice, then it *was* real, even if only within me.

I should mention at this point that I am no mystic in the usual sense of the word; I do not dwell upon the supernatural. The nature of my work, with its relentless schedule and constant deadlines, requires that I be a pragmatist. In other words, I don't usually plunge beyond those things that can be grasped through my senses. When speed is needed, I hurry. When it is not, I wait. I anticipate the needed and avoid the unnecessary. In that regard, I lean toward the demands of civilization.

But there are moments that are set beyond the normal, everyday range of experience. Somewhere I suspect there are things

So, it seemed, the mountains and the trees were offering me a message. But not in rolling thunder from a nearby peak. This was not the place or time for bombastic drama, and the message was not one to be shouted from the treetops. The voice of the wind did not bellow but simply spoke.

"Welcome back," it seemed to say.

"Back from where?" I asked.

"From where you've been."

"Where have I been?"

"Away from the sense of things. You drifted as you became older, more practical. It's a drift that happens to most people."

"Okay. Then why am I hearing your voice now?"

"Because you are ready to hear me."

"But I'm no different now than I was yesterday or last week or even last year."

"Not so."

"What?"

"Not so. Now your senses are attuned."

The allegorical quality of the situation struck me.

"My senses are fine, thank you. And until now my hearing has been perfect," I responded, as I succumbed to an urge to indulge in some teasing, perhaps even mockery. I was playing the game, whatever it was. I seemed to hear a note of mockery in the reply as well as a strong sense of assurance.

"Senses are simply combined perceptions. Now you can perceive the substance of your questions, all your questions. The voices that join in me become the inquisitor you have always sought. What you hear borne on the wind is the representation of all the unknowns that plague your life; the university of life, of love, of fear, of peace that you have not heeded, even denied. This voice embraces all levels of understanding and springs of a

wisdom as old as the mountains before you. Without the fullness of the senses that this experience embodies, you will never come upon the universal understanding that makes men complete; you will be victimized by false wisdom, doomed to gadgetry, to convenience, to your own prepackaged lifestyle. The voice in your ear stands as the last bastion of defense against an aimless search."

I started to ask who spoke, but I knew the answer because it lay before me in the moonlight and the shadow, in the snow and the ice and in the stillness through which the wind-carried voice set up echoes in my mind. The truth was there and here. Part of me had spoken to another part. One level of awareness had touched another.

Out of all that, whether fanciful or mystical, I understood some things I had never understood before. Now I knew that there are no answers, and if there were, they would be valueless. Any answers would be as lacking in substance as the voice that breathed its message into my ear. Answers, to *anything,* are impossible to find. The only value is in the question and the quest for it. In fact, *that* is as close to an answer as I shall ever come. *The quest is the answer.*

And that is why I was here in the first place.

Slowly, I turned back and glided down the gentle slope from the ridge. The others were waiting at the bend of the trail, seemingly unaware that I had gone on a personal errand. Had I been gone minutes or only milliseconds? I did not know. I gave myself a mental shake and looked again at the area in which we stood.

Marshall Lake seemed almost to glow with a light of its own under the moonbeams. The nearby mountaintops were iced with white, and the stars sparkled around them like candles twinkling on an enormous cake. Perhaps the

A young elk finds the approach of skiers near Apollinaris Spring (Yellowstone) a bit too close for comfort.

Sawtooths were celebrating something of their own, and we were the guests looking on with delight. If so, it was time to bid the party good night and head for waiting sleeping bags and the approach of another day.

In the morning, a blue sky greeted us — a carryover from the clear night before. The air was crisp and the aroma of bacon and eggs frying was tantalizing. It was not long before breakfast had vanished and we were donning parkas for what was planned as a fairly casual day. The area offered several good ski bowls and an opportunity to practice some cross-country techniques.

As we skied off from camp, a trio of coyotes could be heard yapping near the lake's edge, and Marshall Peak poked its way above the nearby ridge. A high wind swirled snow off the peak, sending veils of it across the jagged edges of the mountain. In the distance a few new clouds could be seen blowing our way. A 600-foot climb carried us over another ridge and into the chain of bowls.

Without hesitation, we zig-zagged our way up and down the sweeping bowls. It was not difficult skiing. Even climbing to the top of each bowl posed little problem, and we were able to chart a course back to camp that would offer a series of downhill swings. Every now and then we would pause and survey the changing scene. The view changed from bowl to bowl, and part of the fun came from simply taking in the different sights.

The wind had been rising steadily, and it was clear that another storm was headed our way. We viewed it as good news. What we hoped for was a good old-fashioned Idaho snowstorm that would leave a foot or two of powder in its wake. Our only concern was that we not be caught too far from camp in a really big storm, so we began our run back to the hut with dips and glides and sudden rushes that built up momentum for the flat stretches. As we glided into the camp area, the storm that had been lurking around the edges of the nearby peaks burst upon us. The visibility plummeted to almost zero as the sky dumped its own avalanche upon our shoulders. There was little doubt that we would be snowed in for the rest of the day.

The confinement offered its own opportunities. The canvas bunks in the hut were in need of repair. In some places the fabric had torn, and anyone rolling onto one of those bunks ran the risk of an abrupt drop to the hard ground below. We used heavy twine to reinforce the bunks so that no one need fear a sudden and unpleasant awaking in the middle of the night. We also took on the task of stripping all the wax from the skis. The fresh snow that was falling would require a new wax in the morning. Stripping wax is always a chore, but anticipation of good snow conditions in the coming day helped make the work seem easier. Once that was done, we carefully reassembled our gear for what was to be our last full day in the mountains. The packs were repacked, and everything was put in order for an easy, early start in the morning.

With the preparations finally concluded, twinges of cabin fever began to set in. Fortunately, there was an antidote. As no trip into the mountains can be considered complete without at least one good card game, we pulled out a dog-eared deck and settled down for a cutthroat game of Hearts.

For a brief moment I considered sharing my experience with the wind-carried voice atop the ridge with my friends. But they would have taken it to be capricious, I am certain. They may even have searched each other's eyes, asking half-humorously if perhaps cabin fever had struck with unusual swiftness and whether their deranged companion should be restrained for his own good.

And at this point I didn't really care what anyone else might think about it. What I thought about it was all that mattered. It was still an intensely personal experience that

The Sawtooth Mountains rise ahead as a pair of cross-country skiers begin a day trip.

I didn't really feel I should share with anyone. Next week or next month, Maryann could share it with me, but only after I had had a chance to relive the experience. On the other hand that might take a long, long time, and I might want to share it before reaching that goal. But for now I wanted to keep it to myself.

My thoughts were broken by the slap of cards upon each other as the first hand was dealt. Now, the concerns were more immediate. I had a reputation as a card player to maintain, and it was time to look at my first hand.

The game see-sawed back and forth and ran well into the night. Finally we turned in, with the snow-laden wind howling around the tent and our dreams filled with scenes of the fresh powder and clear skies we were anticipating by morning.

The pristine beauty of a winter wonderful enfolds a cross-country skier following a fresh snowfall.

We got half of our wish. A full foot of fresh powder lay on the ground as dawn broke with grey and cloudy skies. We quickly cleared the snow away from the entrance to the hut and soon were enjoying our last batch of bacon and eggs. The final round of packing did not take long, thanks to our preparation the night before. For once there was no question about what kind of wax we would use. We rubbed on a hard green wax for the base and added some blue on the kicker to make climbing easier. Then we shouldered our packs and took off.

Initially we climbed an abrupt 500 feet above Marshall Lake to top out on a ridge that would be our guide for much of the day. The snow conditions were perfect, and the packs on our backs seemed much lighter as our skis skimmed through the powder. This was the kind of snow we had come to find. Ahead, a grouse—startled by our approach—burst from under a snow-covered branch and scooted across our trail.

The first two miles of the trip sped by almost before we noticed they were past. Then we rounded a bend and burst out onto the edge of an enormous bowl. The slopes plunged several hundred feet down to a surrounding ring of pines. In a moment we swung our packs from our backs and dumped them into the soft snow with a splash. A moment more and our skis were slicing downward in a series of Telemark turns that sent the snow spraying out behind in a giant plume. This was skiing!

For the next two hours, we carved our tracks across the virgin snow. The bowl was vast, and there was no way that we could test all its curves and corners. Challenging the steepest slope, my skis gained speed at a startling rate. The approaching tree line became a green blur, and the need to make a turn became imperative. But what might have been a terrific stem christie was converted into a spectacular spill. The result was an unexpected burst of aerial acrobatics ending in a mushrooming splash of snow

that cushioned the fall so that the only injury was to my pride. And even that wasn't too badly dented.

But all good things must come to an end, and we were committed to reaching Stanley by nightfall. Reluctantly, we picked up our packs and pointed our skis down Fishhook Ridge.

For those who tour the Sawtooths, this is one of its most scenic sections. The route along the top of the ridge gives ever-changing views of most of the peaks that make up the Sawtooth range. The trail itself is relatively simple and affords ample opportunity for gawking at the grandeur of what has been labeled the American version of the Swiss Alps.

Reminiscing for a moment, I wondered if the wind might not stir itself one last time and bring my "other" voice for some farewell message, were we to linger on past nightfall, but no sooner did the thought flicker across my mind than I knew the answer. The wind might come, but the voice *never* would again. The timeless, priceless message had been delivered. I did not need to hear it again. Now I could walk, run, or sleep through life without the fear of missing any of it. The great mysteries of the ancients were now no more than sketches on an open pad. Now my personal mystery was my own book. I could open the pages to it. No one else could.

We paused for lunch beside a lightning-blasted, wind-warped old tree. Salami, cheese, and some cookie crumbs uncovered in the bottom of a bag made up our last meal on the trail. The fresh mountain water washed it all down like cold white wine. The last frame of film was snapped, and the cameras were put away as we tightened down the packs for the long, easy run down the ridge and across a meadow to a waiting ranger station.

We glided smoothly through a grove of aspens and then descended into the woods once more. As we worked our way to the lower elevations, the delightful powder turned into wetter snow, but it still was fresh and pleasant for skiing. The trail took a final series of twists and turns and threatened us with several possible spills as a reminder that the trip might be almost over but nature could still spring some surprises. Then the meadow appeared before us, and we could hear the sound of highway traffic in the distance. Civilization, at least in the form of Stanley, was near and so was the end of our trip.

That night, following a full dinner, we soaked for two hours in a hot pool surrounded by snow. The temperature in that natural bath was close to 100 degrees, and it soothed the stiffness out of muscles that had struggled up ridges and plunged down the Sawtooth slopes. The pool was quiet and the sky so close that each star stood out to be counted. But we were counting memories instead. Six days and five nights in the mountains—they had sped by all too rapidly. The next morning would see us aboard a sleek jet for the flight back to Los Angeles. For a last moment, we joined with the spirit of the high country and made a pledge to return. We felt we would be welcome.

Fundamentals of
Cross-Country Skiing

Striding Out

Although we strongly recommend either personal or group lessons for the beginning skier, cross-country skiing is one of the few sports that can be self-taught to a reasonable degree. As a general rule this does not apply to advanced techniques, so we do not attempt here to provide instruction in some of the more advanced turns or other fine points. It is our hope that the information and advice that follow will provide some guidance in basics for both the beginning skier and for the downhill skier who want to try cross-country touring.

The basic stride (usually called the "diagonal stride") is the foundation upon which cross-country skiing rests. It is very similar to the movements used in ice or roller skating, especially in the flow of motion from the feet to the shoulders as the rhythm of the skiing stride develops.

When starting out to learn the basic stride, it is essential to begin in a flat area such as a field or meadow. The snow should not be especially deep, crusty, or wet. An ideal time for starting is the day following a relatively light snowfall that has provided a fresh coating of dry powder snow over an existing base.

Initially, forget about the poles. Put them aside in a convenient place, and concentrate only on the skis. Cross-country ski bindings attach only the toes of the boots to the skis, leaving the heels free to rise and fall with the stride of the skier. The advantages of this arrangement will quickly become apparent.

An ideal time for starting
is the day following a relatively light snowfall
that has provided a fresh
coating of dry powder
snow over an existing
base.

Standing upright on the skis, slowly begin shuffling forward—first with one ski and then with the other. Using this basic shuffling movement, slowly carve a large circle around the field or meadow while you gradually get used to balancing yourself on the narrow skis. As you continue slowly in this shuffling movement, bend your knees slightly so there is a spring in your legs as you shuffle and push one foot ahead of the other in a steady left-right pattern.

Once this movement begins to feel comfortable and natural, in your next circle around the track you have created, try swinging your arms in a natural motion as though you were walking rather than shuffling on skis. You will notice that your left arm swings forward as you slide your right foot forward, and vice-versa. This natural swing of the opposite foot and arm is the basis of the cross-country skiing stride. It establishes the rhythm that can keep a skier going for miles without tiring. For the next few circles around the track, concentrate on developing a rhythmic shuffle that has the right foot and left arm swinging forward, followed by the left foot and right arm.

This natural swing of the opposite foot and arm is the basis of the cross-country skiing stide. It establishes the rhythm that can keep a skier going for miles without tiring.

Once this begins to feel comfortable—and it soon will—it is time to start stepping out a little. Now, instead of a shuffle, try striding forward with your feet. You don't have to take long strides, but there should be a distinct stepping motion, as opposed to the shuffle. So as not to confuse you, a word of explanation is in order about the term *stepping motion* when used in this connection. Normally, a nonskier would relate this to walking—lifting one foot completely off the ground, moving it forward in midair, then placing it back on the ground one stride ahead of the point at which he lifted it. To the skier, *stepping motion* means merely lifting the weight of one foot off the ski and propelling the ski ahead. Rather than

70

lifting your foot high enough to bring the ski off the snow, you merely take enough weight off it for the ski to slide effortlessly ahead. Your arms should be swinging briskly and freely in rhythm with your feet, and your stride will begin to flow over the snow. Your heel comes up off the ski as your weight swings onto the ball of your foot, first one foot and then the other.

At this point you are approaching the "kick-and-glide" technique that takes much of the work out of cross-country skiing. Here, again, the work *kick* can be misleading to those unfamiliar with skiing terminology. It does not mean "kicking" in the same way that your foot leaves the ground to goal a ball. It is, instead, more of a vigorous push of your foot against the ski. As your pushing foot extends back, your heel will rise up off the ski so that the final thrust comes from the ball of your foot. At the same time, your weight will transfer to your other leg, where your knee is partially bent, so that foot rests flat upon the ski. Stated another way, as the pressure or *kick* of your right leg goes down and back, your weight transfers to your left leg to create the glide that carries you over the snow with minimal physical effort. Many skiers, especially racers, spend years polishing and perfecting this technique.

By now you should be beginning to get the feel of it, but you would do well to continue to traverse your circular track until you develop a true sense of the rhythm of the kick-and-glide technique. With repeated practice these motions will feel increasingly natural until they develop into a series of reflex actions that you can perform as automatically as you walk or peddle a bicycle.

Once this basic technique begins to feel comfortable to you, you should take a short break. At the end of the rest period, it is time to pick up the ski poles and bring them into action. You have purposely avoided using them up to

With repeated practice these motions will feel increasingly natural until they develop into a series of reflex actions that you can perform as automatically as you walk or peddle a bicycle.

now so that you don't get off to a bad start by developing a strong dependence on them for balance. Later, even after you develop considerable agility on skinny skis, it's a good idea to put them aside from time to time and practice without them in order to avoid becoming over-dependent on them for maintaining balance. At a later date, when you are out on a real ski trek, there is a chance that you may lose, bend, or break one or both of your poles. Such occurrences are rare, but they do happen. If you have not developed the ability to maintain balance and navigate without them, you could be in for real trouble. You will quickly discover the vitally important role that your ski poles play in cross-country skiing.

This time as you resume your kick-and-glide motion, which should feel a bit more comfortable by now, you will find the poles improving your balance on the narrow skis and making the skiing even easier by biting into the snow and assisting the thrust of your legs as you skim across the meadow. You will soon discover the advantage of using poles is twofold. You can use them not only to take some of the leg work out of skiing, but by combining the full thrust of both legs and poles, you can vastly increase the speed with which you glide over the surface of the snow. Eventually it will all become natural for you. The tip of your ski pole will dig into the snow as your leg delivers its kick to send you skimming over the frozen earth.

By the second or third time out, practicing what you have taught yourself so far, it should all come so easily that you will feel like you have been doing it all your life. Each movement will become part of an overall motion that carries you almost effortlessly over the field of snow. And best of all, there is the feeling of accomplishment in the knowledge that you taught yourself entirely on your own!

By the second or third time out, practicing what you have taught yourself so far, it should all come so easily that you will feel like you have been doing it all your life.

Climbing Up

Of course, skimming across a flat meadow is only part of the skiing technique. As a cross-country tourer, you will not be using a lift or tow to get to the top of a hill or even to the top of a mountain. In fact, one of the advantages of Nordic over Alpine skiing is that there are no expensive lift or tow tickets to buy and no lines at the base of the slope in which to wait — and wait — and wait. The cross-country skier gets to the top of the slope by his or her own muscles. Bear in mind that ski lifts are limited to the most popular — and therefore most populated — ski slopes at highly developed winter resorts. The ultimate goal of those who ski tour for fun and relaxation is to escape such trappings of modern civilization.

Climbing a hill, or even the side of a mountain, while wearing skis is not as difficult as it may sound. If the slope is relatively gentle, it is a surprisingly easy matter to walk right to the top. The secret lies in the combination of proper waxing (which is fully outlined in chapter 9) and of proper skiing technique.

Initially, it is important to keep moving once the walk up the slope has begun. If you simply stop in your tracks halfway up a slope, you may well find yourself in the embarrassing situation of sliding backwards. This is no way means that you must press on beyond the limits of your wind or physical stamina. If it seems wise to stop for a brief rest on the uphill climb, do so by turning your skis sideways so that they are resting perpendicular to the downhill slope or fall line of the hill. At this point, your ankles will be more comfortable if you simply stomp your skis down against the snow so that they dig deeper into it on the uphill side. In this way you will in effect be standing straight up even though you are on an inclined surface, and this will prevent the backward slide. Experienced skiers develop the knack of being able to stop for a rest with the skis in almost any position. Mastery of this technique will come to you from experience and practice, so it is pointless to give it more than passing mention here.

The technique involved in walking up the slope is relatively simple. Just as in the case of the kick-and-glide technique, alternate feet and arms are used in the stride. As you move your right ski forward and upward, dig the left pole into the snow, and vice versa. There is, however, little actual gliding unless the slope is extremely gentle. In most cases you will not skim over the snow but will instead plant your slis firmly with each upward step. The actual step resembles the slapping of each ski against the snow. For example, lift the left ski slightly and move it ahead in a short stride. As it comes back down onto the snow, slap the section of ski beneath your foot and slightly ahead of it lightly against the surface. This helps the wax to grip as your weight is transferred forward onto the ski. At the same time, plant the right pole firmly in the snow approximately even with your left foot while your weight remains tilted slightly forward. Then repeat the process with the opposite ski and pole. Almost before you realize it, you will find yourself moving right up the hillside.

With practice, it is possible to walk up some surprisingly steep slopes without a great deal of difficulty. There are, however, slopes on which this walking approach simply doesn't make sense. For these slopes other techniques have been developed that you will find amazingly simple to learn and master with a bit of practice.

One method of hill climbing is called the "herringbone," for reasons that are obvious when you look back at the pattern of the ski tracks it leaves. In this approach spread the tips of your skis apart so that they make a wide "V," with one ski slightly uphill from the other. Turn the inner edges of both skis down so that they bite into the snow alongside both skis roughly in line with your feet. Advance each ski forward and upward a step at a time, with the edges digging into the snow. While it is simple and effective, you will soon find this approach to be quite tiring. It is, therefore, generally used only for climbing short, steep inclines.

A slower, though infinitely less fatiguing approach to hill climbing is known as "sidestepping." The name itself pretty well describes the technique. To perform it simply place your skis horizontally across the slope perpendicular to the actual incline. In this attitude you simply move up the hill one step at a time just as if you were climbing sideways up a flight of stairs. If the snow is crusty or the slope is unusually steep, you can dig the ski edges into the snow with each upward step to provide a better grip. Here again, the trick is simply to use alternate skis and poles in order to maintain your balance and develop a climbing rhythm that will soon make the going easier than it sounds.

There is another climbing technique that most skiers prefer to use whenever possible because it is usually quicker and consumes infinitely less energy. This popular approach is known as "traversing," and it requires the frequent use of a special, rather simple turn known as the "kick turn." What traversing means is simply cutting diagonally back and forth across the slope rather than trying to go straight up. Set out on an angle of ascent that seems

With practice, it is possible to walk up some surprisingly steep slopes without a great deal of difficulty.

75

comfortable, and simply zig-zag your way up the hill in a pattern similar to a road snaking its way up a steep incline. Often you will find that the traverse technique will permit you virtually to ski up a slope rather than walking or climbing up it. On gentler slopes you will usually discover that you can use your kick-and-glide technique quite easily and effectively.

When it is time to switch from a "zig" to a "zag" in order to continue your uphill progress, simply step the skis around gradually into the new direction and continue on up. Looking down from the top, your trail will resemble a series of connected "Z's."

On steeper slopes or when trees or heavy brush become obstacles, you may find it necessary to use a kick turn to switch your direction. You should first practice the kick turn at least a half-dozen times on level ground before you try it on the side of a hill. It permits you to make a full 180-degree turn while standing in one spot. In this sense it is an awkward but essential maneuver.

In order to learn this technique, you should begin by standing with both skis parallel. Next, kick the downhill leg (this can be either leg when practiced on level ground) forward and up so that the tip of that ski comes up vertically and the trail of the ski clears the ground. Then swing this uplifted ski around so that its tip points back toward the tail of the ski upon which you are balanced. Then lower the ski to the snow, parallel to the one on which you are standing but heading 180 degrees in the exact opposite direction. At this point your knees will be bent in opposite directions. Finally, shift your weight down onto the recently reversed ski and lift the other ski and swing it around until it parallels the other and both skis are facing in the same direction, which is directly opposite to the one in which you had been heading. In performing this admittedly tricky turn-about, be careful not to get your ski tips hung up in shrubs or bushes. You should use your poles to maintain your balance during the change in direction and move them along appropriately with the turning technique. Once you are facing in the opposing direction, you can again take off up the hill.

In our own experience, we must admit that the kick turn sounds more difficult than it really is in practice. In the beginning you may trip yourself a few times or get a bit tangled up in your skis, but with continued practice the movements involved to execute it properly and gracefully will become familiar. Once you really get involved in cross-country skiing, you will quickly learn that the kick turn will become an old and useful friend.

When you have mastered these basic techniques of hill climbing on skis, you will find that most slopes are readily accessible to you. Any thought of taking a power lift to the top will soon lose all its appeal, as it would take half the fun out of the activity. You will learn to appreciate and enjoy the feeling of accomplishment that comes with getting to the top entirely under your own power and by your own ingenuity. Each new slope will appear to you as a fresh challenge to be met, and each summit attained will represent one more challenge that has been overcome.

Now you know how to get to the top of the hill. Of course, getting back down is another matter and involves still another set of techniques.

Now you know how to get to the top of the hill. Of course, getting back down is another matter and involves still another set of techniques.

Skiing Down

For someone who has never done any skiing, the first run down a slope—no matter how gentle—is a frightening experience. From the bottom it looked like an overgrown mole hill. Now that you are on top, it looks like you have suddenly been asked to ski down Mount Everest. As you start down, you will have the feeling that your skis are about to take off on their own and never come to a stop. After that comes the fear of falling. Fortunately, a fall on cross-country skis is seldom serious, and everyone has done it. Usually it hurts nothing but your pride. When it happens to you, as it will, here is a helpful hint: instead of cursing your clumsiness, laugh at it. This will make the going easier and a lot more fun.

The first rule is to start with as gentle a slope as you can find and just get used to the idea of gliding down it on skis. Because Nordic skis are not as wide as Alpine skis (which are designed primarily for downhill or slope skiing), balancing on them during the downhill run is a bit more difficult, but you will soon get the knack of it. Some instructors recommend making the downhill runs with one ski slightly ahead of the other. From our experience, for the most part, that is not really necessary. Such a position is of value only when skiing in deep powder snow that may be lying over hidden gullies—a condition

For someone who has never done any skiing, the first run down a slope —no matter how gentle —is a frightening experience. From the bottom it looked like an overgrown mole hill. Now that you are on top, it looks like you have suddenly been asked to ski down Mount Everest.

that most skiers encounter only rarely. In the beginning you should concentrate on keeping the ski tips more or less even and your weight equally distributed on the skis. Don't try anything fancy. Just try to get from the top to the bottom without falling. Let the poles trail at your sides and concentrate on riding your skis over the snow.

Because you will be somewhat nervous about the first few downhill runs, you will probably have a tendency to tighten up. Try to avoid being too stiff; you should try instead to stay loose. Your legs should be slightly bent so that they will flex easily as the skis skim over any bumps on the slope. This flexed knee action accomplishes the same purpose on skis that springs and shock absorbers do on wheels. Your weight should be thrust slightly forward so that your skis don't run away from you, and your skis should be separated enough so that they are about even with the sides of your hips. You should practice over and over on a gentle slope until you develop confidence while gliding downhill.

Once you have gotten used to the feeling of skiing downhill, there are two basic maneuvers that as a Nordic skier you will need to master. One is the "snowplow," and the other is the "step turn." There are, to be sure, many other advanced techniques, but you can forget about them until later on. For now these two basic maneuvers are the only essential ones you will need to master.

The snowplow is aptly named, as it is performed by creating a wedge in which you push out the tails of your skis, making the tips of both skis angle inward. It is a relatively simple maneuver to master. In use it slows your forward rate of travel much as an automobile's brakes do, simply by increasing friction. In your early attempts at it, the only thing you'll really have to be careful about is to keep the tips of your skis from crossing. If they do, we can guarantee that you're in for an instant spill.

80

The wider the angle of the skis in the snowplow maneuver, the more your forward speed will be reduced. Increasing the width of the arch between your skis works exactly the way applying more pressure to the brake pedal does in driving your car. To decrease your speed still further, dig the inside edges of your skis in against the snow. You can do this simply by pivoting your ankles inward. Just as with the width of the "V" between your skis, the deeper you dig the inside edges of both skis into the snow, the faster your speed will decrease and you will come to a stop. Increasing both of these angles of attack at the same time is equivalent to jamming the car's brake pedal all the way to the floor in a panic stop. As you will soon learn, the snowplow maneuver is effective only at relatively slow speeds on the downhill run. It is, consequently, a technique you will find yourself relying upon heavily during your early cross-country skiing experiences.

Once you are satisfied that you have mastered the knack of using the snowplow maneuver to slow down and even to stop, you will be ready to learn to adapt it to effect a turn or change in direction of travel. In this application it will prove effective even at higher speeds. You will soon find it invaluable in emergency situations such as breaking away from a downhill plunge or bringing yourself to a complete stop at higher speeds. To execute this turning maneuver, utilize the same basic snowplow technique, except now do not dig the edges of your skis into the snow but keep them flat against the surface. If you want to turn to the right, angle your left ski somewhat more sharply than your right one, and shift some extra weight over to that ski. At the same time, point your legs and feet more toward the right, and you will find yourself going smoothly into the right turn. To make a left turn, simply reverse the process. In practice this maneuver will allow you to effect a skidding turn in whichever direction you wish to go. While you will

In the early stages of learning period, bear in mind that you must not try to make the turns too fast. Slow down before attempting to negotiate a turn. The thing cross-country skis are neither intended nor designed to handle high-speed maneuvers like those associated with their downhill cousins.

find that getting the hang of the snowplow turn will come easily to you, a word of caution is in order. If you shift your weight too abruptly onto one ski, it can cause that ski to turn out from under you, and down you will go.

Throughout your use of the snowplow, it is essential to maintain a wide stance, with your skis well apart. Such a position will provide you with both increased control and a greater sense of security while you are learning to negotiate turns on skis. An added advantage of the wider stance is that there will be less chance of inadvertently crossing the tips of your skis while you are in this position. In the early stages of your learning period, bear in mind that you must not try to make the turns too fast. Slow down before attempting to negotiate a turn. The thin cross-country skis are neither intended nor designed to handle high-speed maneuvers like those associated with their downhill cousins.

The step turn is likely to be your most frequently used maneuver for changing direction while going downhill. You will find this especially true at higher speeds. Fortunately. it is a relatively easy maneuver to master. We would recommend, however, that you first practice it on a comparatively flat area.

The best approach is to find a gentle slope that bottoms out into a long glide across a flat stretch of snow. Use a short, straight downhill run to gain momentum. As you reach the flat stretch, place all of your weight on one ski (the left ski if you are turning right and the right ski if you are turning left), and the lift the other ski just slightly off the snow. Next, rotate the tip of the lifted ski to an angle in the direction in which you want to go. Place it back on the snow, and transfer your weight over onto it. Don't make the angle too sharp. Finally, bring the first ski back in line with the ski on which you are now gliding and continue on your way. It is better to use several short step turns rather than to try for a single large one. It will be easier on your legs and easier on your skis. Through practice and experience, you will soon discover that it will often take several step turns to set the exact course you want.

You can also use the step turn maneuver simply and effectively to bring yourself to a stop. All you do to accomplish this is to continue to make a series of turns until you are heading uphill. Then you will simply glide to a stop. The pull of gravity serves as your automatic braking system.

The step turn is a quick and easy technique for avoiding small obstacles that may appear in your path, to simply change direction, as well as to extend a run across a downhill slope.

Traversing has already been discussed as a means for climbing up a hill. Its greatest attribute is that it effectively takes one steep slope and divides it up into a number of gentle ones. In climbing up a hill, it takes much of the hard work out of the climb. In skiing down the hill, it removes the fright and danger of making a steep, fast descent before you are prepared to handle it. Simply zig-zag your way down in a pattern of connected "Z's." In this way you cut back and forth across the angle of the slope, making the descent in as many easy steps as you like. Keep a wide stance between your skis, and keep the uphill ski about a foot ahead of the downhill ski. If the slope is quite steep, simply snowplow to a stop at the end of each leg of your descent, use a kick turn to reverse your direction, and continue on down the slope at whatever pace you set for yourself. An alternative is to use the step turn in an uphill direction to come to a stop, then a kick turn to reverse direction. The fall line of the hill you are descending will determine which stopping technique is most suitable.

As continued practice and experience brings you from the level of a beginner to that of an intermediate skier,

*From our own experi-
ence, even extended
backpacking trips into
the wilderness seldom de-
mand much more than
the basics we have just
described.*

you will begin to notice many more experienced skiers using advanced techniques such as the various "christies." While these originated with the Alpine slope skiers, many of them can be successfully performed on cross-country skis as well. When you feel that you are ready to learn these techniques, it is vitally important that you seek competent professional instruction. Essentially, these are simply advances on the basic techniques. They are impressive and showy, but most cross-country skiers out for a recreational day or weekend will find little need for them.

With the snowplow and the step turn, the average cross-country skier is well equipped to meet most of the challenges he or she is likely to encounter in a day of casual touring on skinny skis. From our own experience, even extended backpacking trips into the wilderness seldom demand much more than the basics we have just described.

Avoiding Spills

Spills on skis are much like automobile accidents in that most of them could be prevented by simply remaining alert. Common causes of both are distraction, absent-mindedness, and not paying attention to the course ahead when traveling at relatively high speeds.

When skiing with partners who fall behind, there is a great temptation to turn around to check on them. Resist it. Call back and listen for an answer, or slow down and wait for them to catch up and come alongside you. If you attempt to make a turn to see if they are all right, you may turn right into their pathway.

There are many beautiful views and unfamiliar sights in the great outdoors under its blanket of snow. To take in these beauties and see all these strange sights is part of the great appeal of cross-country skiing. That is what you are there for, so by all means enjoy it. See and feel and hear the marvels of unspoiled nature. But before you get carried away with it all, stop. If you were driving a car at 60 miles an hour and spotted a beautiful scene, you would pull over to the side of the road, stop, and enjoy it; otherwise you would be inviting disaster. Exercise this same caution while skiing. Even out in the wilderness, collisions are not as uncommon as you might believe.

Until you have gotten so much skiing experience under your belt that it is second nature to you, it is wise to give

Spills on skis are much like automobile accidents in that most of them could be prevented by simply remaining alert. Common causes of both are distraction, absent-mindedness, and not paying attention to the course ahead when traveling at relatively high speeds.

Out in the quiet open space of the wilderness, away from the usual distractions that keep us alert, there is a form of autohypnosis that can very easily set in.

the attitude of your skis a visual check now and then. Are they parallel, too close together, or angled in to where they could easily overlap?

Perhaps the most prevalent cause of spills is absent-mindedness, but not the type associated the the proverbial jokes about the professor. Out in the quiet open space of the wilderness, away from the usual distractions that keep us alert, there is a form of autohypnosis that can very easily set in. The beauty, the peace of mind, and the feeling of being close to nature can create an euphoric state that lulls the conscious area of the mind into an hypnotic state, allowing the subconscious to express itself. In this state your inner awareness is greatly heightened and you sort of drift into a kind of metaphysical meditation. You can feel this state of mind as it begins to develop. Stop and rest and let it take over. It is a wonderful experience and is good for the body, the mind, the emotions, the spirit. While your inner consciousness, or what some people call the subconscious mind, is in high gear, your conscious mind is inoperative. If you don't stop and rest until the mood passes, you could run smack into a tree with your eyes wide open. This is closely akin to the hypnotic effect that passing headlights have on the person who tries to drive after he should have stopped, or to the driver who gets so enmeshed in a daydream that he is totally unaware that he is driving a car.

The Skinny Skis

A lot of people—especially downhill skiers—look at cross-country equipment and say, "Oh, no. Not me. Not on those flimsy looking things!" And, at first blush, you might think they have a point. Certainly, the equipment is very light and contrasts sharply with the traditional pattern of heavy skis and boots. The latter have long dominated Alpine skiing. However, the cross-country skier is not out to duplicate Robert Redford's role in "The Downhill Racer." And that makes a big difference.

The real key to much of cross-country skiing is lightness. The "skinny skis" are longer and narrower than their Alpine counterparts and they weigh much less. The lightness of the equipment is an important reason for the sport not being as demanding or as hard work as some people might otherwise think. After all, who wants to haul around twenty or thirty pounds of skis, boots, and bindings on their feet all day.

It was not always this way. The man who now looms as the Red Grange or Babe Ruth of cross-country skiing— the remarkable John "Snowshoe" Thompson—used very heavy equipment. Thompson carried mail, medicine, and gossip over the Sierras from 1856 to 1876. One of his better known routes ran from Placerville, California, over Echo Summit and through Luther Pass to Genoa, Nevada.

There are dozens of Snowshoe Thompson stories and many people have different favorites. One that is popular [and, perhaps, apocryphal] involves a meeting between Thompson and a pack of wolves. In those days, wolves were still plentiful in the Sierras.

In no way were Thompson's skis a model for today's cross-country gear. A native of Telemark, Norway, Thompson made his first skis based on childhood memories. They were eleven feet long and weighed twelve pounds each. Later, he cut down somewhat on the length and weight by using skis that were only nine feet long. And he didn't use the type of ski poles you see today. Not by a long shot. Old Snowshoe carried a six-foot pole and he used it more for balance than anything else. He had another interesting habit. Snowshoe didn't ski around small cliffs. He just jumped off of them. And, in all his years of carrying the mail, he never suffered an accident.

There are dozens of Snowshoe Thompson stories and many people have different favorites. One that is popular (and, perhaps, apocryphal) involves a meeting between Thompson and a pack of wolves. In those days, wolves were still plentiful in the Sierras.

The long day was winding its way toward evening and Thompson was beginning to give some thought to where he would spend the night. He usually bedded down in empty caves or abandoned cabins and, when those weren't available, he just wrapped himself in his blankets and curled up next to the campfire. In any event, old Showshoe rounded a curve and saw gathered in front of him a pack of hungry wolves. Any wolves seen in the Sierras during winter were assumed to be hungry and, while Thompson may have been thinking about dinner, he wasn't planning on becoming a meal himself.

As the distance between himself and the assembled wolves narrowed, Thompson decided on a bluff. He let out a loud yell and hurled himself forward on his big, heavy skis. Still accelerating, he hurtled past the four-legged congregation, which stared at him in stunned amazement. In another moment, he was safely around bend and well on his way with no sign of pursuit from the wolves. A close call had provided another story for him to tell at the end of his run.

Today, you not only don't have to worry about wolves but you also don't have to lug around those heavy skis. Depending on their nature and intended use, touring skis range in weight from three pounds to six pounds. Racing skis are even lighter and mountaineering skis may be heavier. But, for the moment, let's talk about the light touring and general touring skis.

There is a continuing and unresolved argument about which ski is better for the beginner—light touring or general touring. As the name implies, the light touring ski is markedly lighter and more narrow than the general touring ski. It has more flex to it and provides a better "feel" for the terrain over which you are skiing. However, it is somewhat harder to balance on than the general touring ski and some people—especially those used to the much wider Alpine skis at the downhill resorts—are put off by this fact.

The wider and heavier general touring ski makes balancing easier and is a better all-around work ski. However, it is stiffer than the light touring ski and lacks the other ski's "feel" of the terrain. On the other hand, it is certainly the ideal ski for longer trips where carrying a pack may be involved. And it is generally more sturdy.

So, you say, which should you get? Well, that calls for a two-part answer. For the beginner, the light touring ski seems the best bet. Sure, balancing may be a little more difficult at first. But the lighter ski provides a better sense of the technique and movement involved in cross-country skiing and, in the long run, will make you a better skier. The second part of the answer is that for the more experienced skier the general touring ski meets a broader range of needs. On a long trip or in rough terrain, the general touring ski is preferable.

There is a continuing and unresolved argument about which ski is better for the beginner—light or general touring.

It used to be that all of the cross-country skis were made of wood. Generally, they were laminated hickory with hard edges of lignostone. The majority of cross-country skis still falls in that category. But the more expensive fiberglass skis are coming on strong because of their lightness and durability. In fact, the fiberglass ski may soon dominate the field.

Now, most skis require waxing—a subject to be discussed later—but some do not and there are degrees of waxing. The traditional wooden skis must be pine tarred on the bottom to seal out moisture that would otherwise ruin the ski. Pine tarring can be a chore and, while most wooden skis still require it, changes have come along that could make pine tarring obsolete. The important change is the development of the synthetic base. Let it be quickly said that some synthetic bases are better than others and it definitely pays to check them out. The synthetic bases still require waxing but do not require pine tarring and, in some cases, do not even require a base wax but simply the appropriate running wax for whatever the current snow conditions.

Then, there are the no-wax skis. For the most part, they either utilize a plastic "fish scale" base or a pair of mohair strips along the center of the ski. These enable you to climb without sliding backward but tend to be less effective than waxed skis when it comes to gliding. For the very occasional skier who doesn't want to be bothered with learning about waxing, these skis are fine. But waxing technique is a very real part of cross-country skiing and one develops a certain pride in being able to wax properly.

Frankly, despite a definite growth in the popularity of no-wax skis, we must declare a prejudice in favor of the fiberglass or wooden skis with the synthetic bases. The purists will shout that you should go all the way with pine tarring and everything. But that really is not necessary. The synthetic bases permit the joys of waxing without the mess of pine tarring. They make cross-country skiing fun without detracting from its basic nature.

SKIER'S			RECOMMENDED	
Height		Weight	Ski Size	Pole Size
Cm. = Ft. in.		Lbs.	Cm.	Cm.
90	3'		100	75
100	3'3"		110	80
110	3'7"		120	85
115	3'9"		130	90
125	4'1"		140	95
130	4'3"		150	100
135	4'5"		160	105
140	4'7"		170	110
145	4'9"	100	180	110-115
155	5'1"	115	190	120
160	5'3"	130	195	125
165	5'5"	140	200	130
170	5'7"	150	205	135
175	5'9"	160-180	210	140
180	5'11"	160-180	210	145
185	6'1"	180-200	215	150
190	6'3"		To	155
195	6'5"	200 +	220	160

Ski Length is determined by the skier's weight and height. If a person is heavier or lighter than average, skis should be one size longer or shorter respectively.

Pole Length is determined from the floor to mid-shoulder. For mountain touring, poles may be somewhat shorter.

As their names imply, racing skis and mountaineering skis are more specialized. The racing skis are unsuited for any other purpose and many mountaineering skis are designed for really rugged treks that most cross-country skiers are unlikely to confront on a regular basis. The Fischer Europa 77 combines the metal edges and ruggedness of most mountaining skis on what is essentially a general touring fiberglass ski. It is a personal favorite for almost all touring conditions.

The boom in cross-country skiing has produced a surge of developments in all equipment, especially in the manufacture of the skis. The fiberglass revolution in cross-country skiing has arrived and even further advances seem almost certain.

Waxing Enthusiastic

Now, a few words about waxing. As is probably very clear by now, you may have figured out that waxing is important in cross-country skiing. In fact, some Nordic skiers take great pride—perhaps inordinate pride—in their waxing skills. Some even make a mystery out of the process, as though some snowy spirit had whispered the proper instructions in their ear. Pay no attention to such nonsense. It is not really that big a deal.

If you are using one of the no-wax skis, the question of waxing doesn't even arise. But, if you are like most people and are using a ski that requires waxing, don't panic. Proper waxing is easily learned and requires only practice and a little common sense to perfect the technique.

No comments on waxing would be complete, however, without a horror story. At least the following one has a point to it. One sunny morning at Mt. Pinos in the Los Padres National Forest north of Los Angeles, two college students arrived in their shiny yellow foreign car. It was a clear, crisp day, and the snow had been deposited quite recently. The two women got out of their car and began smearing the bottoms of their skis with red klister. Red klister has the consistency of freshly chewed bubble gum, and the women were laying it on about 1/4 inch thick. The stuff is to be used only under adverse wet snow conditions. But the man who rented them their skis had told them it would keep them from sliding backwards. It certainly did. It also kept them from sliding forward. By the time they got the sticky stuff stripped from their skis, their day was pretty well ruined.

The moral of the story is that with the tremendous boom in cross-country skiing, there are a lot of people renting or selling the equipment who don't know their base wax from their klister, and their advice is worse than useless. As a result beginning skiers often find themselves overwhelmed by the apparent difficulties of waxing. So let's take a look at what really is involved.

If you want to learn how to put wax on, take a how-to-do-it book and a ski and go practice. What follows is for thinking about *before* you start waxing.

Waxes are made by many manufacturers and vary tremendously. Some of the newer waxes, such as Jack Rabbit, are considerable departures from the more traditional brands. Some now even come in spray cans. All waxes, however, are designed to cover two basic conditions. One is snow that is cold, with a temperature below freezing; the other is snow that has warmed up beyond the freezing point and is turning wet. The colder the snow, the harder the wax you must use; the wetter the snow, the softer the wax until finally you reach the stage of using the sticky klisters.

In most cases the klisters should be used only as a last resort. Some people, however, tend to use them as a crutch in place of better technique when snow is in a transitional phase. In other words, people put the klister wax on too soon on the theory that it will make climbing easier. It may, but it slows down the glide and really is something of a cop out.

The traditional waxes, which are the waxes most widely available, are color coded, and they all have instructions on the side of the can or tube detailing what

94

snow condition the wax is designed to handle. As a general rule of thumb, remember that cold snow won't pack when you scoop it up, while transitional snow packs beautifully into a firm ball and wet snow oozes the water when you pack it.

Most wax manufacturers offer a basic package of three waxes that are fine for starting out. They cover the middle range of snow conditions, and a competent salesperson should be able to discuss their merits with you. Rental packages usually include similar wax kits. It is a very good idea to start out with one of the major wax brands such as Swix, Rex, or ToKo and stay with it until you are familiar with all the varieties it provides. Because the waxes are not identical, mixing brands can lead to confusion. If you stay with one brand, selecting the proper wax soon becomes almost automatic.

Just as the side of the tube or can usually carries a description of the snow conditions that the particular wax is designed to meet, so it includes directions for applying the wax. If it doesn't, however, the dealer should be able to give you quick instruction, as it really is not difficult. A mistake commonly made is to avoid waxing the ski altogether, then climbing aboard right away and taking off over the snow. The proper technique is to wax the ski, then lay the ski bottom down on the snow for at least 10 minutes to give the wax time to adjust to the temperature of the snow. Even then, unless it is glaringly obvious, don't assume right away that you have applied the wrong wax just because your skis may be slipping a bit. Ski on them for a little while before changing waxes. Give the wax a chance to adapt itself to the snow.

Cross-country poles and bindings are pretty standard. Just remember that the poles should come to near the top of your shoulders and the bindings should match your boots. Make sure the binding clamps the boot down

Most wax manufacturers offer a basic package of three waxes that are fine for starting out. They cover the middle range of snow conditions, and a competent salesperson should be able to discuss their merits with you.

95

tightly at the toe. Otherwise, you will have serious control problems.

Boots, however, are a little more complicated. There are two basic types of boots. One is the low-cut boot that looks something like a track shoe or tennis shoe. It is lightweight and works beautifully for recreational cross-country skiing or racing. The other type is the somewhat stiffer high-top boot that comes up over the ankle. It is designed for more varied touring over mountainous terrain. It provides firmer support that is most welcome on a long trip.

It is almost impossible to overstress the importance of having boots that fit properly. If they are too loose — especially at the heel — your ski control will be diminished. If they are too tight, they will hurt your feet. The thing to bear in mind is that you are going to be skiing (which means standing) in those boots for some time. Finding a pair that fits is well worth whatever investment in time and money that may be required.

Covering Up

People often ask about what clothing to wear for cross-country skiing. Until recently, the answer placed the emphasis more on comfort than on style. But now, much to the delight of clothing manufacturers, Nordic skiers are becoming more style conscious. We suspect there is a direct correlation between that and the impact of increased advertising, as a similar relationship may be found in the higher prices being asked for cross-country ski clothing.

One of the real advantages of cross-country skiing, however, is that the demands of fashion have not taken the sport over yet. Hopefully, they never will. As a result, almost any clothing that is appropriately warm and comfortable will do. It is not unusual to see people who are out for a pleasant day of skiing wearing simply blue jeans and a sweater.

The traditional Nordic skiing outfit consists of long wool socks, corduroy or wool knickers, and a warm, long-sleeve shirt or sweater. There are, however, infinite variations. Obviously, what you wear will depend on the weather and the kind of ski touring you have in mind.

The real secret is to dress in layers. In other words underwear, shirts, pants, a light sweater, and a parka or jacket made of 60/40 cloth should do the job most of the time. As the day warms up and the exercise of skiing generates body heat, you can remove the outer layers and stuff them in a small day pack for use later. On a warm day, even at very high altitudes, it is not unusual to see people skiing in no more than a pair of gym shorts. But you should always be on guard against chilling. Remember that when you stop for a rest, you will notice the cold much more quickly.

There are three items you should make sure to *always* carry—good sunglasses, a warm hat, and gloves. Sunglasses are very important because of the protection they provide against snow blindness. The glare of the sun shining on the snow is extremely bright, much brighter than you might realize while you are skiing. When skiing in deep powder or in stormy weather, it is a good idea to have snow goggles. Under good conditions, you won't need them, but they can be invaluable in bad weather, as they keep wind-blown snow out of your eyes so that you can ski without being half blind.

The hat and gloves are important because of the protection they provide against unnecessary chill. Because they get less blood, the hands, like all extremities, are more subject to chill and even frostbite than other parts of the body. On warm days most people dispense with gloves, but when the temperature starts to drop, gloves effectively help stave off the cold. Incidentally, unless it is very cold, gloves work much better than mittens.

A hat is necessary for preserving warmth and can really help guard against hypothermia. Exposed skin loses heat quickly, and your head offers a great deal of exposed skin; hair provides only scant protection. Perspiration evaporates rapidly from the head and leads to rapid cooling. As a result, the body sends more blood to the head at the expense of other areas. Clearly, a wool knit hat is an important item that should not be overlooked.

Down clothing has long been popular with downhill skiers and winter outdoor enthusiasts. It is, however, expensive and for the most part unnecessary for cross-country skiers unless overnight conditions of severe cold are expected. It is true that nothing beats down for warmth; nonetheless, most cross-country skiers find that dacron fiberfill usually meets their needs in insulated clothing. Although dacron is not as efficient as down when it comes to insulation, it resists the effects of moisture much better; it dries out more rapidly than down, and when wet it retains some of its insulating quality.

These are those who insist that gaiters — water-repellent cotton or nylon tubes that attach to the boot and come in both ankle and knee lengths — are essential for cross-country skiing. The idea is that they keep snow out of your boots and off your legs and therefore help prevent the chill caused by wet feet or wet socks. In very deep or wet snow, they can be valuable, but under most conditions a good pair of boots that fits snugly around the ankles and good woolen socks are more than adequate.

Most skiers prefer to wear two pairs of socks. The first pair is a short cotton or wool liner of medium weight that comes up over the ankle just like a sweat sock. The long, wool knee-length socks go on over the liners. Not only is this warmer, but it also helps reduce the chance of developing blisters.

Finally, there is one item that is not really clothing but should always be carried: suntan lotion or sun screen. Just as the glare of the sun on the snow makes sunglasses essential, so it makes protection against sun and wind burn necessary. To forget it is to guarantee yourself some painful rather than pleasant skiing memories.

There are three items you should make sure to always carry—good sunglasses, a warm hat, and gloves. Sunglasses are very important because of the protection they provide against snow blindness.

99

Chowing Down

Skis, bindings, boots, poles, waxes, and essential clothing—a list that includes almost everything you need for a day of fun in the snow. Now you are ready to skim over the meadows, glide through the forests, walk up a hillside and race down a gentle slope, right? Well, almost.

Actually, we have covered all of the basic equipment and techniques you will need for a day of casual ski touring. The next subject, however, is one of perpetual interest: food and drink.

After a full morning of cross-country skiing, even if it is only a case of plowing back and forth across a meadow and up and down a few gentle slopes, there is one thing of which you can be certain: you are going to be both hungry and thirsty. How do you meet the demands of a rumbling stomach and dry throat? The answer, like most in cross-country skiing, is fairly simple.

First, let's take a look at the possibilities for liquid refreshment. Obviously, if you have brought a portable stove along, you can boil water and have hot chocolate, coffee, or tea. But that really seems to be overdoing it unless you are on a longer tour. It is much easier to carry a plastic bottle of a cold drink. While we do not usually recommend specific brands, sometimes we make exceptions, as in the area of food. For example, there is broad agreement among skiers that Wyler's powdered lemonade and Tang powdered orange drink meet the requirements of thirst quenching, energy supply, and ease of carrying and preparation better than most others.

After a full morning of cross-country skiing, even if it is only a case of plowing back and forth across a meadow and up and down a few gentle slopes, there is one thing of which you can be certain: you are going to be both hungry and thirsty.

On a day tour, it is best to mix your drink in a plastic water bottle and hang the bottle from your belt or tuck it into your day pack. A cloth pouch that slips onto your belt and carries either pint or quart size plastic bottles is very handy. Should your drinking supply get too warm, just drop some clean snow into it. That suggestion may produce shouts from some about possible contamination, as any form of water that falls through the atmosphere is less than totally clean. But dumping a little snow into a quart of lemonade to cool it off rarely does any harm, and if you are hot and thirsty, the temptation to cool the drink off with snow is going to be virtually irresistible anyway. During a longer break, such as lunch, burying the drink bottle in the snow is an effective cooling method.

Once you have quenched your thirst, what about food to ease the pangs in your stomach? You should think in the terms of items that are easily carried and easily digested. For lunch most experienced Nordic skiers carry a hunk of cheese—Swiss, American, longhorn, cheddar, or whatever you like—and another hunk of meat. The meat usually takes the form of salami, summer sausage, or something similar. Add a knife for slicing the cheese and salami, and you have a handy luncheon package. It is not fancy, but it is convenient and filling, and it certainly tastes good when you are hungry.

Of course, there are many ways of adding variety without adding too much extra weight. Some people like to carry a fresh orange along to nibble for desert. Others recommend highly a carton of fruit yogurt or an apple. Some toss in a hard-boiled egg or two, and others prefer jerky or the dried fruit and nut mixture inelegantly dubbed "gorp." Use your imagination. If it sounds good to you, try it.

On a longer trip, the basics remain the same. The lunch package really doesn't vary much, but you do have to consider additional items for breakfast and dinner, and this is where warm food enters the picture.

Of course warm food requires cooking and you have two choices: you can build a campfire in the snow, or you can use a portable stove. Campfires are a lot more fun, and when the necessary materials such as dry wood are available along with the proper conditions, they are worth the extra effort. The basics of campfire building in the winter are similar to those in summer, but there are some differences. Use dry wood and plenty of small twigs to get your fire going, but don't build the fire under snow-covered branches. Find a level area and use your skis and then your boots to pack the snow into a firm platform base. Then use large pieces of wood to form a platform to keep the fire above the snow. The fire will still sink into the snow, but it will do so much more slowly. Beyond this, campfire building is much the same regardless of season.

Even if you think you will be able to build a campfire, you should carry a portable stove with you as a precaution. After all, conditions may not be right for building a campfire. In addition, the stove is easier to start and cooks the food much faster, and there are times when you will not want to spend a lot of time with a campfire.

There are two basic choices when it comes to portable stoves. You can use stoves that burn white gas or that burn butane. Propane stoves generally are too heavy for use on a long ski trip. Both white gas and butane stoves can present some cold-weather problems, and the choice is largely a personal one. With the development and improvement of the Gerry-type butane stoves, however, we tend to lean toward butane. Unless you want to go to the exceptional and expensive Mountain Safety Research stove, which burns almost any fuel under almost any conditions. Whatever your choice, don't forget the water-

Of course warm food requires cooking and you have two choices: you can build a campfire in the snow, or you can use a portable stove.

103

proof matches.

As to the food, hot chocolate, coffee, or tea can provide the essential liquid nourishment, and dehydrated foods will meet the needs of breakfast and dinner. Actually, a little packaged oatmeal or one of the hot cereal mixes that are now available in the supermarkets will do quite nicely for breakfast, along with Tang or whatever you prefer as fruit juice.

Dehydrated food doesn't have to taste like cardboard, and it doesn't have to cost as much as your neighborhood camping store might charge. Research has shown that labels such as Richmoor and Dri-Lite tend to be more expensive at a camping supply center than at a neighborhood supermarket. This is not to say that the brands sold in the camping stores aren't good; some are excellent. But dehydrated and freeze-dried food sold in supermarkets is usually cheaper and often quite tasty. Tea Kettle freeze-dried foods are very good and can be found both in camping stores and in supermarkets. The powdered Lipton soups also are lightweight and excellent, as are the Cup of Noodles packages and many others that can be found on the supermarket shelves.

Winter cooking is much simpler than summer cooking at a campsite in at least one sense: there is a plentiful water supply. All you have to do is boil the snow. One thing worth remembering, however, is not to fill your pan full of snow when you try to melt and boil it. What happens is that the snow on the bottom melts and boils away while the snow on top remains. It is most effective to add a little snow at a time until your pot is full of boiling water rather than trying to do it all at once. As is so often the case in the wilderness, a little patience can save a lot of time and effort.

Backpacking Stoves

WHITE GAS

Caution: Do not use automotive fuel

Advantages / **Disadvantages**

Advantages	Disadvantages
Spilled fuel evaporates readily	Priming required
Stove fuel used for priming	Spilled fuel very flammable
Fuel readily available in U.S.	Self-pressurizing stoves must be
High heat output	insulated from snow or cold

KEROSENE

Spilled fuel will not ignite readily	Priming required
Stove can be set directly on snow	Spilled fuel does not evaporate
Fuel available throughout the world	readily
High heat output	

BUTANE

No priming required	Higher cost fuel
No fuel to spill	Empty cartridge disposal a problem
Immediate maximum heat output	Fuel must be kept avove freezing for
	effective operation
	Gas cartridges cannot be changed
	until empty
	Lower heat output

ALCOHOL

Lightweight stove	Low heat output
No priming required	High fuel cost
Spilled fuel evaporates readily	Limited control of heat
Stable in wind	

Taking Off

With thoughts of a simmering pot of stew, some hot tea, and a crackling campfire still in mind, this is a good time to take a closer look at the longer cross-country ski tour. Such a tour should not be attempted by a beginning skier, and it helps if those on a longer trip have had some summer backpacking experience. Winter wilderness travel can be hazardous for the unwary and ill prepared. But for those who are ready, a ski tour can be one of the most rewarding wilderness experiences of a person's life.

One of the very first things to do before starting out on a tour of more than a day is to prepare a checklist with two factors in mind: safety and weight. If you overload yourself, you may become overtired, and that presents a serious safety problem. It is possible to pack all you need for a two- or three-day tour and keep the total weight per person to less than 40 pounds. That weight may sound excessive to summer backpackers, but winter gear, especially clothing, simply weighs more than similar equipment for a summer trip.

The accompanying checklist is divided into a section listing personal supplies that each individual should have and a section with group supplies to be divided and used as a basic guide. With experience, nearly everyone develops his or her own priorities in terms of items to be

One of the very first things to do before starting out on a tour of more than a day is to prepare a checklist with two factors in mind: safety and weight.

added or deleted. In addition, weather conditions and the terrain may dictate certain changes.

Some of the items on the checklist, especially those in the first-aid kit, may require some extra effort to acquire. The prescription drugs are a good example. But they can be very valuable, and most doctors will provide you with a reasonable supply once you explain the need for the drugs.

Two other items are optional, but we would not be without them. One is a space blanket, which comes in both a compact and a large size. You should choose the size that suits the circumstances and activity you anticipate. The other item is a camera and, of course, the film to go with it. You can get into a raging debate over which type of film works best when taking color photos under snowy conditions. We'll pass on that except to note that is can be difficult to photograph snow with films that have a blue base. If your camera has a lens that takes filters, be sure to include both a skylight (or ultraviolet) filter and a polarizing filter.

Most of the gear you take along in your pack, which necessitates a few words about packs. Once the tour stretches beyond the one-day, recreational jaunt, it becomes necessary to switch from the day pack to the full-fledged backpack. This will bring about an immediate loss in stability.

Many skiers like the European-style rucksacks, which have a large capacity and a reasonable amount of stability when used with a waistband. Most packs made in the United States, however, are designed around the standard contoured aluminum packframes. These remain the best for long ski treks, but their high center of gravity makes your balance decidedly unstable. The situation can be improved by loosening the shoulder straps and tightening the waistband.

108

Personal Checklist	Group Checklist
Wool or corduroy knickers	Cooking pots (2)
Wool shirt	Stove and fuel
Wool sweater	Tent
Cotton turtleneck pullover	Snow shovel (aluminum)
Windshirt	Water bucket (collapsible)
Wool hat	Plastic ski tips (2)
Gloves	Food (1½ to 2 lbs, per
Wool mittens	person per day)
Wool knee socks	Tent
Wool or combination	Repair kit:
inner socks (2 pairs)	screwdriver
Thermal socks	pliers
Long underwear (2 sets)	ski screws
Down socks (for very	electrician's tape
cold nights)	needles and thread
Parka (down or dacron)	Waterproof matches
Gaiters	Candles
Sleeping bag (down	First-aid kit:
or dacron)	3" Ace bandage
Sleeping bag cover	adhesive bandages
Ensolite-type pad	gauze pads (telfa)
Ski boots	adhesive tape
Skis and poles	safety pins
Wax kit	tweezers
Avalanche cord	antiseptic ointment
Cup	tetracycline
Spoon	aspirin (10gr) or APC's
Pocket knife	salt tablets
Flashlight	soma compound
Personal items	dexadrine
(i.e., toothbrush,	moleskin
soap, suntan lotion,	plastic whistle
etc.)	first-aid handbook
Sunglasses	Wire saw
Paperback book	Cleaning supplies
Maps and compass	(brillo pads, paper
Toilet paper	towels, biodegradable
	detergent, etc.)

Camping Out

Before you swing that large pack onto your back and head for the hills, there is one subject that deserves further attention. Where are you going to spend the night? The summertime practice of tossing the sleeping bag under a nearby tree is out of the question. Either you will have to use a tent, or someone will have to build a snow cave or an igloo. In an event, some sort of shelter is an absolute necessity.

It may seem obvious to say that cross-country tourers should set up camp well before nightfall, but all too often the urge to go just one more mile before calling it a day seems irresistible. Resist it. Setting up camp in the dark is absolutely no fun at all.

Look for a fairly level, sheltered area. If you are below timber line, use the trees as a windbreak. Don't, however, camp directly under the trees, because snow falling from the higher branches can douse your campfire and collapse your tent. It is ideal to have a stream of water running nearby, as a fresh water supply eliminates the time- and fuel-consuming process of melting snow.

Having selected a campsite, the next question is one of shelter. There is no doubt that short of a cabin, a snow cave or igloo is the best, most snug type of winter wilderness shelter. Snow caves require a good slope of well-settled snow, although an alternative can be a large fallen tree that is thoroughly covered with snow. The trunk of the tree can provide a secure wall or ceiling upon which to base your temporary home. In flat terrain the only choice is an igloo.

Digging out a snow cave or building an igloo is not terribly difficult, but it is very time consuming. Be sure the walls are at least a foot thick, and don't forget to poke holes through for ventilation. Also, the entrance to the cave or igloo should be lower than the sleeping level so that when the cold air enters, it can flow down without chilling the people who are sleeping. It is a very good idea to build a practice igloo or dig a practice snow cave in a convenient area before attempting to do so in the wilderness.

The biggest problem with snow caves and igloos is that they require several hours to dig out or build. If you are setting up a base camp for a stay of several days, they are a great idea, but they make very little sense if the campsite is only going to be used for one night. The time and effort needed to create them is just too great for the limited use they would get. Tents can be put up in a matter of minutes and with far less effort.

In fact, it is sheer folly to take off on an extended tour without a tent. Tents provide the surest shelter in the shortest amount of time and can quite literally be the key to survival should conditions suddenly deteriorate. But not all tents are appropriate for winter conditions. You should be cautious because even some that are billed as mountaineering tents fail to meet the tests of winter.

A good tent will be made of light ripstop nylon, which keeps out the wind, yet "breathes" enough to allow some passage of air. There should be ample ventilation and, preferably, two doors. Most winter campers agree that the tunnel or sleeve type door is best.

A cooking hole near the main entrance is also a good idea. The tent should come equipped with snow stakes, unless it is one of the relatively few free-standing tents designed for winter use. The fabric of the floor and the lower part of the sides must be waterproof. The poles should be sectional, made of aluminum, and should fasten to the tent at both the top and the bottom. Otherwise, they will sink into the snow.

An important factor in tent design is that it be big enough so that you can bring your packs and other gear (skis and poles) inside with you. At the same time, it must be lightweight. A good rule of thumb is to assume that the tent should weigh three pounds for each person who is going to use it. Thus, a two-man tent should weigh only six pounds. There are those who argue that the tent should include a rainfly and a frost liner. While they are nice to have—especially the rainfly—and can come in quite handy, practical experience shows that they are frequently set aside because they add to the weight and more often than not tend to go unused. We favor a rainfly but never use a frost liner.

There are a few tenting tricks you should keep in mind. For example, keep your skis on while doing the initial packing down of the tent platform. Then from that base, pack it down even harder with your boots. When setting up the tent, keep the door facing away from the wind. When inside, remember that sleeping bags and other items will stay drier if they do not touch the sides of the tent, where some condensation is certain to develop.

Whether you are in a tent, a snow cave, or an igloo, it is certain that you will be using a sleeping bag, and there can be no argument that the best and lightest sleeping bags are filled with goose down. They are, however, also the most expensive. Fortunately, the newer dacron-filled bags are adequate for all but the most severe winter conditions and are much cheaper. In addition, they are much less affected by moisture: dacron retains some of its insulating quality

It is a very good idea to build a practice igloo or dig a practice snow cave in a convenient area before attempting to do so in the wilderness.

even when wet. A good compromise are the fiber-down bags, which feature a down-filled cover on top and polyester batt on the bottom to take advantage of the qualities of both materials.

No matter how good the sleeping bag, it will be of only limited value without an ensolite or other foam pad to separate it from the cold floor. Air mattresses are far less efficient under winter conditions, and no snow camper in his or her right mind would use one. Incidentally, clothing for use the next morning can be nicely warmed by tucking it into your sleeping bag for the night.

Avalanche Notes

It seems as though it has become almost obligatory to include a chapter on avalanches in every book written about cross-country skiing. Avalanches are not much fun to write about, and most experts agree that there is still a lot to be learned about them. As a result information on them can be somewhat imprecise. Frankly, it would be nice just to skip over the subject. But anyone who has ever seen or even heard an avalanche rumbling down a mountain slope and sensed the destruction contained in that sliding mass of snow tends to take avalanches very seriously indeed.

We do not pretend that this chapter is a definitive discussion of avalanches. There are entire books on the subject, and a great deal can be learned simply by talking with ski patrol experts and others who deal with avalanches on a daily basis. Furthermore, avalanche conditions vary widely in different parts of the country. The best thing to do before starting out on any serious mountain tour is to check with the local forest rangers or ski patrol people about the avalanche conditions in the area. It is their job to know them, and their advice is well worth heeding.

Once your trip is underway, the most important rule of thumb to remember is that the greatest avalanche danger occurs during and just after a large snowfall or windstorm. The new snow is unsettled and much more likely to slide. If you encounter a major storm while on a long tour, it is a good idea to simply hole up for a day and give the snow a chance to stabilize. If nothing else, you can practice building an igloo or digging out a snow cave.

The best thing to do before starting out on any serious mountain tour is to check with the local forest rangers or ski patrol people about the avalanche conditions in the area.

The delay may be unwelcome, but it beats getting caught in an avalanche.

Beyond keeping track of storms, learn to identify areas where avalanches are most likely to be found. Old avalanche paths can be identified by shaved-off trees and cleanly swept slopes where there is little vegetation, for example. Cornices are notoriously dangerous avalanche triggers and should be avoided as much as possible. In the wet snow that is so common during spring skiing, the presence of rolling "snowballs" indicates unstable snow. Open slopes are more hazardous than heavily timbered slopes. Windward slopes are usually safer than lee slopes simply because of the buffeting they get from the wind, but there is never a guarantee of their safety.

If you must ski across a potential avalanche area, never do so by yourself.

If you must ski across a potential avalanche area, never do so by yourself. In fact, the more people you have around, the better. Each skier should make the crossing separately while under the watchful eyes of other members of the party and should also follow in the tracks of his or her predecessor, making sure to tie on his avalanche cord and spread it out in the snow. The cord—50 feet of brightly colored, light nylon line—will usually remain visible even if a person is buried in an avalanche. Before starting, remove the ski pole straps from your wrists so that your hands will be free should you be caught in an avalanche.

If you are caught, make every effort to stay upright. It will take much more snow to bury you if you are upright than it will if you fall down. Keep both hands near your face and chest, and as you come to a stop, cover your mouth with one hand while thrusting the other one straight up toward the surface. Keep an air space open around your face, and if you are thoroughly trapped, stay still. Try to avoid burning up oxygen with wild efforts. Preserving air will give your companions more time to locate you and get you free of the snow.

If a companion is caught in an avalanche, move as quickly as possible to rescue the victim. Time is of the essence. Someone who has been buried in an avalanche has less than a 50-50 chance of surviving unless he or she is found within a hour. A rapid search is vital to a companion's survival.

Look immediately for any traces of the victim at the spot where he or she was last seen. Be alert for skis, gloves, and especially the avalanche cord. Begin probing. You can use the heels of your skis or the ski poles, if the baskets are removable. All members of the party should form a line and push their probes into the snow in front of them, then move forward a step at a time and repeat the process until the victim is located. It is generally better to launch an immediate search than to rush off for extra help. The time lost getting help could turn out to be critical to the victim. If you are in a well-patrolled area, however, one member of the party can go for help while the others search.

All this is not intended to give the impression that an avalanche lurks around every mountain corner, just waiting to snare the unwary. If that were the case, mountain touring would lose its appeal in a hurry. Avalanches do present a real danger in the mountains, but reasonable care can circumvent the threat. A few basic precautions can minimize the danger and result in a maximum amount of fun.

So now you are all packed. Your tent, sleeping bag, skis, food, and other gear are in good shape. Hopefully, you are too. Your checklist has been checked. The weather reports have been studied, and you know the snow conditions. Two days, three days, perhaps a week lies before you. The meadows, mountains, and forests are waiting. It's time to tour.

Beyond keeping track of storms, learn to identify areas where avalanches are most likely to be found.

117

Where To Go

As we have mentioned, any place you find snow can be the place to go cross-country skiing. It can be around the corner or over the next hill or even next door. There are, however, some special areas worthy of mention — the national parks and forest lands. Because they are federally supervised and the federal administrators are under steady pressure from conservationists, these areas include large sections of wilderness that is virtually untouched, especially in winter.

The national forest lands have been used by Nordic skiing enthusiasts for several years, and some of the best cross-country ski schools are located on or near such land. The national parks have been slower to develop as cross-country ski areas but are now clearly climbing on the bandwagon. An exception is the magnificent Yosemite National Park in California's Sierra Nevadas, where one of the oldest, biggest, and best cross-country ski centers is located. The Yosemite center pioneered Nordic skiing in the national parks.

More recently other national parks have joined the parade. They include the heavily visited Yellowstone National Park, its southern neighbor Grand Teton National Park, the unique Lassen Volcanic National Park, Glacier National Park, where the avalanche hazard may be the highest, and Zion, Bryce Canyon, and Acadia National Parks, among others. These parks have thus far proved to be the most popular, although there are others worth exploring on skis.

The national forest lands have been used by Nordic skiing enthusiasts for several years, and some of the best cross-country ski schools are located on or near such land.

Entertainer Roger Miller once wrote a song entitled "You Can't Roller Skate in a Buffalo Herd." Well, you can't ski in one either, but you can come pretty close. The secret is to do your cross-country skiing in the nation's oldest national park — Yellowstone.

There are several hundred bison (more commonly known as American buffalo) in the park, but most summertime visitors get to see only a handful. Sometimes weighing as much as 2000 pounds, they are the biggest animals in the park, and during the summer they usually retreat to the higher meadows beyond the reach of the casual visitor. In winter, however, the huge creatures drift lower and lower as the snow piles itself deeper and deeper at the higher elevations, within easy reach of the cross-country skier.

Yellowstone was first established as a park in 1872, but for the most part the first snows of winter usually chase people out. As a result, Yellowstone is primarily thought of as a summer park. For the cross-country skier, the "summer park" image is a real blessing. During the summer months the park is jammed with visitors. Winter, however, brings a new solitude. Once the snow has fallen, it is possible to ski all day in the park without seeing another person. The only reminders of civilization are occasional telephone lines and the jet trail of an airplane overhead. Those who want to get away could ask for little more.

The cross-country skier in Yellowstone will find himself or herself seeing far more animals than people. The animal scene in winter, however, differs somewhat from the summer picture. For one thing, the bears disappear. There are two species of bear in Yellowstone — grizzly and black bear — but because the bears spend much of the winter in their dens, a skier gliding across the snow is not apt to see them. Their tracks, however, may be spotted from time to time, along with those of bobcats and cougar. Following animal tracks through the fresh snow can be fun as well as educational. It is possible to follow one of the cats to where he caught his breakfast and read the entire story of the hunt spelled out on the surface of the snow.

Of course, there are many other animals around as well. Elk are the most common of the large animals in the park. There are about 13,000 of them, and they frequently are found near the rivers and streams and around the thermal areas. Less plentiful and much more solitary are the moose, the largest of Yellowstone's deer family. Spotting these ungainly animals is more often a case of luck than anything else. The winter snows, however, help drive them down to areas more accessible to the cross-country skier. Bighorn sheep, coyotes, and other animals also are plentiful, and the park's enormous bird population provides continuous entertainment from daybreak to dusk.

One condition unique to Yellowstone should be mentioned. The thermal areas, which are the sites of the famed geysers, hot springs, and pools, put on a tremendous winter display. Their heat, however, melts the snow, and an unwary skier can suddenly discover that his trail has become mud covered rather than snow covered.

Because of its gentle terrain and sloping contours, Yellowstone offers a wide variety of skiing opportunities, as well as an extraordinary range of wildlife and the fascinating phenomena of the thermal areas. The park's neighbor to the south, Grand Teton National Park, offers much of the same in addition to the nation's most awesome mountains.

The Grand Teton National Park literally has to be seen to be believed. The rugged block-fault mountains leap up 7000 feet from the flatlands below. Grand Teton itself tops out at an elevation of 13,770 feet, and the neighbor-

Winter, however, brings a new solitude. Once the snow has fallen, it is possible to ski all day in the park without seeing another person.

121

ing peaks brush impressively close to that cloud-scraping altitude.

Until the coming of the fur trappers in the early 1800s, humans carefully avoided the area during the winter months because of the bitter cold and the deep snow. Probably the first white man to enter this area was John Colter, who arrived in the winter and then pushed north to discover the wonders of Yellowstone. Ironically, when he returned to civilization, most people refused to believe the stories he told about the area. On cross-country skis, it is possible to see the Tetons as Colter saw them.

It is important to note that winter in the Tetons is a genuine wilderness experience. It is here that the famed Snake River begins its long and rugged journey to the Pacific Ocean. Access to the river is easy, and skiing beside it is a pleasant adventure with ample opportunity to view wildlife.

As in Yellowstone, wildlife in the Tetons is plentiful during the winter, and people are relatively scarce. Both elk and moose often can be seen, and it is not unusual to have a curious coyote play tag with you for a mile or more. An easy game can develop as you try to see how close you can get to your four-legged companion. The coyote makes the rules, however, and the skier who tries to get too close will find that the game is quickly over and the partner is gone.

Other national parks provide tremendous skiing opportunities, and the fact that we have not discussed them individually doesn't mean that they are not worthwhile. Each is special in its own way and should be enjoyed to the fullest. But Yellowstone and Grand Teton together offer such a unique combination of beauty and accessible wildlife that any volume dedicated to the delights of cross-country skiing must pay special respects to these parks.

It's Ski Time

If you have stayed with us this far, then you may be prompted to take advantage of the next snowfall and stride out on those long, skinny skis. With a snowy cushion beneath your feet, you can go almost anywhere you wish. The more familiar you become with cross-country skiing techniques, the further you can go and the wider and more varied your opportunities for exploring and enjoying the winter wilderness will be.

With the exception of those parts of the country where snow seldom falls, almost anywhere in the United States offers a cross-country skiing area. A snowstorm can transform a scraggly, frost-browned meadow into a skier's paradise within a few hours. Less than a foot of snow will convert a muddy forest trail into a smooth touring track. With a light snack tucked into a day pack or even into jacket pockets, the cross-country skier is on his or her way.

Just pick your place. Even the Midwest offers ski-touring opportunities. In fact, the sport has been known in the Midwest for many years. With the substantial Scandinavian heritage, especially in Minnesota, Wisconsin, and Michigan, Nordic skiing is nothing new there.

The fact that the Midwest is a little short on mountains and, therefore, a little short on downhill skiing opportunities has also helped to focus attention on cross-country techniques. Many areas now use special cross-country tracks that set a course across the flat, snowy fields and allow the skier to concentrate on his technique and meet man-made challenges that the local terrain may not offer.

A similar approach to Nordic skiing is also found in the East, especially in up-state New York, New Hampshire, and Vermont. Such areas as Lake Placid and Glens Falls in New York, Putney in Vermont, and Hanover in New Hampshire all have a supply of cross-country tracks.

Yet the East also offers a chance for some dramatic ski touring. The White Mountains of New Hampshire, for example, offer a superb Alpine setting that is justifiably famous for its spring ski-touring opportunities. And there are, of course, the Berkshires, the Catskills, most of the Adirondacks, and other, gentler ranges. The wet and bitter cold of the Eastern winter adds an extra challenge that skiers in other parts of the country seldom experience.

Nordic skiing in the United States has rolled like a snowball from east to west and made a substantial splash in the Rockies — those massive, rugged peaks that have been the delight of downhill skiers for years. Names like Alpine and Vail have long been associated with downhill runs, but recently they have added Nordic ski schools and guide services that have rapidly proven successful. In Colorado an organized ski hut system exists, and there are many old miner's cabins to be found and used for shelter.

There is, however, one drawback to the Rockies in the winter. Because of the nature of the weather and the winter snowfall, the threat of an avalanche to the skier who tours away from an established area is very real. But this danger eases in the spring, and the Rockies also afford thousands of opportunities for spectacular Nordic skiing without the avalanche danger, as the Great Teton and Yellowstone National Parks show.

124

The Pacific Northwest still remains a stronghold of Alpine skiing, and the maritime climate, with its wet and heavy snowfall, can make Nordic skiing difficult. Again, there is an avalanche hazard. Nonetheless, cross-country skiing is becoming very popular in the area. Volcanic peaks, such as Mt. Baker, Mt. Hood, Mt. Adams, and Mt. Ranier all offer good areas for ski touring, and ski excursions into the Cascades are on the increase. To the south, of course, are the extraordinary Sierras.

So there it is. From national parks to back yards and most places in between, the opportunity to enjoy winter on cross-country skis is almost limitless. Whether your taste runs to the mountains or the meadows, to the forests or the fields, the joys of cross-country skiing are within your reach. It is even *good* for you. Citing the many skiers in their seventies and eighties and even nineties, one enthusiast was heard to exclaim that it is a sure way to pursue a healthy old age.

But the real truth is that it is just plain fun. It doesn't have to be fancy or expensive, and you can set your own pace. Somehow the sky seems bluer and the white clouds fluffier when you are skimming over the snow. The worries of the everyday world drop away as cast-off cares that have no place in the wonderland of winter touring.

Well, what are you doing still reading this book? Put it down on the coffee table, pull yourself up out of your easy chair, beg, borrow, rent, or even buy some skinny skis and head for where the snow lies piled around the tree trunks or draped over a meadow. A bright, enchanting winter world awaits you.

About the Authors

Dan Blackburn works as a correspondent for the NBC Radio Network News. His articles have appeared in the Saturday Review, *the* Nation, McCalls, Coronet, Pageant, *and* Viva, *as well as in many major newspapers. Maryann Jorgenson, his wife, is a broadcast engineer for CBS.*